FIX-IT and FORGET IT

WEEKNIGHT FAVORITES

FIX-IT and FORGET-IT®
WEEKNIGHT FAVORITES

Simple & Delicious Family-Friendly Meals

127
Instant Pot®
& Slow Cooker
Recipes

HOPE COMERFORD

Photos by Bonnie Matthews

Good Books

New York, New York

Good Books books may be purchased in bulk at special discounts for sales promotion, corporate gifts, fund-raising, or educational purposes. Special editions can also be created to specifications. For details, contact the Special Sales Department, Good Books, 307 West 36th Street, 11th Floor, New York, NY 10018 or info@skyhorsepublishing.com.

Good Books is an imprint of Skyhorse Publishing, Inc.®, a Delaware corporation.

Visit our website at www.goodbooks.com.

10 9 8 7 6 5 4 3 2 1

Library of Congress Cataloging-in-Publication Data

Names: Comerford, Hope, author. | Matthews, Bonnie, photographer.
Title: Fix-it and forget-it weeknight favorites : simple & delicious
   family-friendly meals : 127 Instant Pot and slow cooker recipes / Hope
   Comerford ; photos by Bonnie Matthews.
Other titles: Weeknight favorites
Description: New York, New York : Good Books, [2024] | Series: Fix-it and
   forget-it | Includes index. | Summary: "127 Instant Pot and slow cooker
   meals to make dinnertime a breeze"-- Provided by publisher.
Identifiers: LCCN 2023041725 (print) | LCCN 2023041726 (ebook) | ISBN
   9781680999051 (paperback) | ISBN 9781680999112 (epub)
Subjects: LCSH: Pressure cooking. | Electric cooking, Slow. | Quick and
   easy cooking. | One-dish meals. | LCGFT: Cookbooks.
Classification: LCC TX840.P7 C53 2024 (print) | LCC TX840.P7 (ebook) |
   DDC 641.5/884--dc23/eng/20230919
LC record available at https://lccn.loc.gov/2023041725
LC ebook record available at https://lccn.loc.gov/2023041726

Cover design by David Ter-Avanesyan
Cover photo by Bonnie Matthews

Print ISBN: 978-1-68099-905-1
Ebook ISBN: 978-1-68099-911-2

Printed in China

Contents

Welcome to Fix-It and Forget-It Weeknight Favorites

We get it. The daily question of "What's for dinner?" can be tiresome, monotonous, and incredibly frustrating. Some of us get stuck in a major rut! Wandering around the grocery store for hours looking for uncommon ingredients for overcomplicated recipes also isn't a fun option. That's where this book steps in to save your weeknight dinners!

In your hand, you're holding 127 slow-cooker and Instant Pot recipes sure to please every member of your family. One of my favorite things to do is give a cookbook to my kids and tell them to each pick a recipe or two for the week. They *love* being involved, and you'd be surprised at some of the things they're willing to try when they have the option to choose. Let them get involved with the grocery shopping and the assembling too! There are recipes like Cheese Ravioli Casserole, Carolina Pot Roast, Walking Tacos, Jazzed-Up Pulled Chicken, Salsa Lime Chicken, Baby Back Ribs, Stuffed Sweet Pepper Soup, Loaded Baked Potato Soup, and Macaroni and Cheese too!

Throughout this book, you will see icons in the upper right-hand corner to indicate if the recipe is for slow cooker or Instant Pot. Some slow-cooker recipes will have an adaptation to be made in the Instant Pot, and some Instant Pot recipes will include an adaptation to be made in the slow cooker. So, if you see two icons, that's why! See? We're already making this dinner thing as easy and stress-free as possible for you!

If you don't know where to begin, I always suggest reading the book from cover to cover. Learn some new things about your slow cooker and Instant Pot by reading the first few sections. Make some notes in the margin. Put together a grocery list. Then, pick a recipe and give it a go, knowing you're making a recipe that is tried and true!

Now, go grab the appliance of your choice, and cook with love! Your weeknight frustration is finally over.

* **Please note:** all of the Instant Pot recipes in this cookbook are meant for the traditional 6-qt Instant Pot.

Choosing a Slow Cooker

Not All Slow Cookers Are Created Equal . . . or Work Equally as Well for Everyone!

Those of us who use slow cookers frequently know we have our own preferences when it comes to which slow cooker we choose to use. For instance, I love my programmable slow cooker, but there are many programmable slow cookers I've tried that I've strongly disliked. Why? Because some go by increments of 15 or 30 minutes and some go by 4, 6, 8, or 10 hours. I dislike those restrictions, but I have family and friends who don't mind them at all! I am also pretty brand loyal when it comes to my manual slow cookers because I've had great success with those and have had unsuccessful moments with slow cookers of other brands. So, which slow cooker(s) is/are best for your household?

It really depends on how many people you're feeding and if you're gone for long periods of time. Here are my recommendations:

For 2–3 person household	3–5 quart slow cooker
For 4–5 person household	5–6 quart slow cooker
For 6+ person household	6½–7 quart slow cooker

Advantages and Disadvantages of a Large Slow Cooker:

Advantages:
- You can fit a loaf pan or a baking dish into a 6- or 7-quart, depending on the shape of your cooker. That allows you to make bread or cakes, or even smaller quantities of main dishes. (Take your favorite baking dish and loaf pan along when you shop for a cooker to make sure they'll fit inside.)
- You can feed large groups of people, or make larger quantities of food, allowing for leftovers, or meals, to freeze.

Disadvantages:
- They take up more storage room.
- They don't fit as neatly into a dishwasher.
- If your crock isn't ⅔–¾ full, you may burn your food.

Advantages and Disadvantages of a Small Slow Cooker:

Advantages:
- They're great for lots of appetizers, for serving hot drinks, for baking cakes straight in the crock, and for dorm rooms or apartments.
- Great option for making recipes of smaller quantities.

Disadvantages:
- Food in smaller quantities tends to cook more quickly than larger amounts. So keep an eye on it.
- Chances are, you won't have many leftovers. So, if you like to have leftovers, a smaller slow cooker may not be a good option for you.

My Recommendation

Have at least two slow cookers; one around 3 or 4 quarts and one 6 quarts or larger. A third would be a huge bonus (and a great advantage to your cooking repertoire!). The advantage of having at least a couple is you can make a larger variety of recipes. Also, you can make at least two or three dishes at once for a whole meal.

Manual vs. Programmable

If you are gone for only six to eight hours a day, a manual slow cooker might be just fine for you. If you are gone for more than eight hours during the day, I would highly recommend purchasing a programmable slow cooker that will switch to warm when the cook time you set is up. It will allow you to cook a wider variety of recipes.

The two I use most frequently are my 4-quart manual slow cooker and my 6½-quart programmable slow cooker. I like that I can make smaller portions in my 4-quart slow cooker on days I don't need or want leftovers, but I also love how my 6½-quart slow cooker can accommodate whole chickens, turkey breasts, hams, or big batches of soups. I use them both often.

Get to Know Your Slow Cooker

Plan a little time to get acquainted with your slow cooker. Each slow cooker has its own personality—just like your oven (and your car). Plus, many new slow cookers cook hotter and faster than earlier models. I think that with all of the concern for food safety, the slow-cooker manufacturers have amped up their settings so that "High," "Low," and "Warm" are all higher temperatures than in the older models. That means they cook hotter—and therefore, faster—than the first slow cookers. The beauty of these little machines is that they're supposed to cook low and slow. We count on that when we flip the switch in the morning before we leave the house for ten hours or so. So, because none of us knows what kind of temperament our slow cooker has until we try it out, nor how hot it cooks—don't assume anything. Save yourself a disappointment and make the first recipe in your new slow cooker on a day when you're at home. Cook it for the shortest amount of time the recipe calls for. Then, check the food to see if it's done. Or if you start smelling food that seems to be finished, turn off the cooker and rescue your food.

Also, all slow cookers seem to have a "hot spot," which is of great importance to know, especially when baking with your slow cooker. This spot may tend to burn food in that area if you're not careful. If you're baking directly in your slow cooker, I recommend covering the "hot spot" with some foil.

Take Notes

Don't be afraid to make notes in this cookbook. It's yours! Chances are, it will eventually get passed down to someone in your family, and they will love and appreciate all of your musings. Take note of which slow cooker you used and exactly how long it took to cook the recipe. The next time you make it, you won't need to try to remember. Apply what you learned to the next recipes you make in your cooker. If another recipe says it needs to cook 7–9 hours, and you've discovered your slow cooker cooks on the faster side, cook that recipe for 6–6½ hours and then check it. You can always cook a recipe longer—but you can't reverse things if it's overdone.

Get Creative

If you know your morning is going to be hectic, prepare everything the night before, take it out so the crock warms up to room temperature when you first get up in the morning, then plug it in and turn it on as you're leaving the house.

If you want to make something that has a short cook time and you're going to be gone longer than that, cook it the night before and refrigerate it for the next day. Warm it up when you get home. Or, cook those recipes on the weekend when you know you'll be home and eat them later in the week.

Slow-Cooker Tips, Tricks, and Other Things You May Not Know

- Slow cookers tend to work best when they're ⅔ to ¾ of the way full. You may need to increase the cooking time if you've exceeded that amount, or reduce it if you've put in less than that. If you're going to exceed that limit, it would be best to reduce the recipe, or split it between two slow cookers. (Remember how I suggested owning at least two or three slow cookers?)

- Keep the veggies on the bottom. That puts them in more direct contact with the heat. The fuller your slow cooker, the longer it will take its contents to cook. Also, the more densely packed the cooker's contents are, the longer they will take to cook. And finally, the larger the chunks of meat or vegetables, the more time they will need to cook.

- Keep the lid on! Every time you take a peek, you lose 20 minutes of cooking time. Please take this into consideration each time you lift the lid! I know, some of you can't help yourself and are going to lift anyway. Just don't forget to tack on 20 minutes to your cook time for each time you peeked!

- Sometimes it's beneficial to remove the lid. If you'd like your dish to thicken a bit, take the lid off during the last half hour to hour of cooking time.

- If you have a big slow cooker (7–8 quart), you can cook a small batch in it by putting the recipe ingredients into an oven-safe baking dish or baking pan and then placing that into the cooker's crock. First, put a trivet or some metal jar rings on the bottom of the crock, and then set your dish or pan on top of them. Or a loaf pan may "hook onto" the top ridges of the crock belonging to a large oval cooker and hang there straight and securely, "baking" a cake or quick bread. Cover the cooker and flip it on.

- The outside of your slow cooker will be hot! Please remember to keep it out of reach of children and keep that in mind for yourself as well!

- Get yourself a quick-read meat thermometer and use it! This helps remove the question of whether or not the meat is fully cooked, and helps prevent you from overcooking the meat as well.

- Internal Cooking Temperatures:
  - Beef—125–130°F (rare); 140–145°F (medium); 160°F (well-done)
  - Pork—140–145°F (rare); 145–150°F (medium); 160°F (well-done)
  - Turkey and Chicken—165°F
  - Frozen meat: Don't put frozen meat into the slow cooker. The meat does not reach the proper internal temperature in time. This especially applies to thick cuts of meat! Proceed with caution!

- Add fresh herbs 10 minutes before the end of the cooking time to maximize their flavor.
- If your recipe calls for cooked pasta, add it 10 minutes before the end of the cooking time if the cooker is on High; 30 minutes before the end of the cooking time if it's on Low. Then the pasta won't get mushy.
- If your recipe calls for sour cream or cream, stir it in 5 minutes before the end of the cooking time. You want it to heat but not boil or simmer.
- Approximate Slow-Cooker Temperatures (Remember, each slow cooker is different):
  - High—212°F–300°F
  - Low—170°F–200°F
  - Simmer—185°F
  - Warm—165°F
- Cooked beans freeze well. Store them in freezer bags (squeeze the air out first) or freezer boxes. Cooked and dried bean measurements:
  - 16-oz. can, drained = about 1¾ cups beans
  - 19-oz. can, drained = about 2 cups beans
  - 1 lb. dried beans (about 2½ cups) = 5 cups cooked beans

What Is an Instant Pot?

In short, an Instant Pot is a digital pressure cooker that also has multiple other functions. Not only can it be used as a pressure cooker, but depending on which model Instant Pot you have, you can set it to do things like sauté, cook rice, grains, porridge, soup/stew, beans/chili, porridge, meat, poultry, cake, eggs, and yogurt. You can use the Instant Pot to sauté, steam, or slow cook or even set it manually. Because the Instant Pot has so many functions, it takes away the need for multiple appliances on your counter and allows you to use fewer pots and pans.

Getting Started with Your Instant Pot

Get to Know Your Instant Pot

The very first thing most Instant Pot owners do is called the water test. It helps you get to know your Instant Pot a bit and might even take a bit of your apprehension away (because if you're anything like me, I was scared to death to use it).

Step 1: Plug in your Instant Pot. This may seem obvious to some, but when we're nervous about using a new appliance, sometimes we forget things like this.

Step 2: Make sure the inner pot is inserted in the cooker. You should *never* attempt to cook anything in your device without the inner pot, or you will ruin your Instant Pot. Food should never come into contact with the actual housing unit.

Step 3: The inner pot has lines for each cup. Fill the inner pot with water until it reaches the 3-cup line.

Step 4: Check the sealing ring to be sure it's secure and in place. You should not be able to move it around. If it's not in place properly, you may experience issues with the pot letting out a lot of steam while cooking, or not coming to pressure.

Step 5: Seal the lid. There is an arrow on the lid between and "open" and "close." There is also an arrow on the top of the base of the Instant Pot between a picture of a locked lock and an unlocked lock. Line those arrows up, then turn the lid toward the picture of the lock (left). You will hear a noise that will indicate the lid is locked. If you do not hear a noise, it's not locked. Try it again.

Step 6: *Always* check to see if the steam valve on top of the lid is turned to "sealing." If it's not on "sealing" and is on "venting," it will not be able to come to pressure.

Step 7: Press the "Steam" button and use the +/- arrow to set it to 2 minutes. Once it's at the desired time, you don't need to press anything else. In a few seconds, the Instant Pot will begin all on its own. For those of us with digital slow cookers, we have a tendency to look for the "start" button, but there isn't one on the Instant Pot.

Step 8: Now you wait for the "magic" to happen! The cooking will begin once the device comes to pressure. This can take anywhere from 5 to 30 minutes, in my experience. Then, you will see the countdown happen (from the time you set it for). After that, the Instant Pot will beep, which means your meal is done!

Step 9: Your Instant Pot will now automatically switch to "warm" and begin a count of how many minutes it's been on warm. The next part is where you either wait for the NPR, or natural pressure release (the pressure releases on its own), or do what's called a QR, or quick release (you manually release the pressure). Which method you choose depends on what you're cooking, but in this case, you can choose either, because it's just water. For NPR, you will wait for the lever to move all the way back over to "venting" and watch the pinion (float valve) next to the lever. It will be flush with the lid when at full pressure and will drop when the pressure is done releasing. If you choose QR, be very careful not to have your hands over the vent, as the steam is very hot, and you can burn yourself.

The Three Most Important Buttons You Need to Know About

You will find the majority of recipes will use the following three buttons:

Manual/Pressure Cook: Some older models tend to say "Manual," and the newer models seem to say "Pressure Cook." They mean the same thing. From here, you use the +/- button to change the cook time. After several seconds, the Instant Pot will begin its process. The exact name of this button will vary depending on your model of Instant Pot.

Sauté: Many recipes will have you sauté vegetables or brown meat before beginning the pressure cooking process. For this setting, you will not use the lid of the Instant Pot.

Keep Warm/Cancel: This may just be the most important button on the Instant Pot. When you forget to use the +/- buttons to change the time for a recipe, or you press a wrong button, you can hit "Keep Warm/Cancel" and it will turn your Instant Pot off for you.

What Do All the Buttons Do?

With so many buttons, it's hard to remember what each one does or means. You can use this as a quick guide in a pinch.

Bean/Chili. This button cooks at high pressure for 30 minutes. It can be adjusted using the +/- buttons to cook more, for 40 minutes, or less, for 25 minutes.

Cake. This button cooks at high pressure for 30 minutes. It can be adjusted using the +/- buttons to cook more, for 40 minutes, or less, for 25 minutes.

Egg. This button cooks at high pressure for 5 minutes. It can be adjusted using the +/- buttons to cook more, for 6 minutes, or less, for 4 minutes.

Less | Normal | More. Adjust between the *Less | Normal | More* settings by pressing the same cooking function button repeatedly until you get to the desired setting. (Older versions use the *Adjust* button.)

Meat/Stew. This button cooks at high pressure for 35 minutes. It can be adjusted using the +/- buttons to cook more, for 45 minutes, or less, for 20 minutes.

Multigrain. This button cooks at high pressure for 40 minutes. It can be adjusted using the +/- buttons to cook more, for 45 minutes of warm water soaking time and 60 minutes pressure cooking time, or less, for 20 minutes.

+/- Buttons. Adjust the cook time up [+] or down [-]. (On newer models, you can also press and hold [-] or [+] for 3 seconds to turn sound off or on.)

Porridge. This button cooks at high pressure for 20 minutes. It can be adjusted using the +/- buttons to cook more, for 30 minutes, or less, for 15 minutes.

Poultry. This button cooks at high pressure for 15 minutes. It can be adjusted using the +/- buttons to cook more, for 30 minutes, or less, for 5 minutes.

Rice. This button cooks at low pressure and is the only fully automatic program. It is for cooking white rice and will automatically adjust the cooking time depending on the amount of water and rice in the cooking pot.

Soup/Broth. This button cooks at high pressure for 30 minutes. It can be adjusted using the +/- buttons to cook more, for 40 minutes, or less, for 20 minutes.

Steam. This button cooks at high pressure for 10 minutes. It can be adjusted using the +/- buttons to cook more, for 15 minutes, or less, for 3 minutes. Always use a rack or steamer basket with this function, because it heats at full power continuously while it's coming to pressure, and you do not want food in direct contact with the bottom of the pressure cooking pot or it will burn. Once it reaches pressure, the steam button regulates pressure by cycling on and off, similar to the other pressure buttons.

Instant Pot Tips, Tricks, and Other Things You May Not Know

- Never attempt to cook directly in the Instant Pot without the inner pot!
- Once you set the time, you can walk away. It will show the time you set it to, then will change to the word "on" while the pressure builds. Once the Instant Pot has come to pressure, you will once again see the time you set it for. It will count down from there.
- Always make sure the sealing ring is securely in place. If it shows signs of wear or tear, it needs to be replaced.
- Have a sealing ring for savory recipes and a separate sealing ring for sweet recipes. Many people report their desserts tasting like a roast (or another savory food) if they try to use the same sealing ring for all recipes.
- The stainless steel rack (trivet) the Instant Pot comes with can used to keep food from being completely submerged in liquid, like baked potatoes or ground beef. It can also be used to set another pot on, for pot-in-pot cooking.
- If you use warm or hot liquid instead of cold liquid, you may need to adjust the cooking time, or the food may not come out done.
- Always double-check to see that the valve on the lid is set to "sealing" and not "venting" when you first lock the lid. This will save you from the Instant Pot not coming to pressure.
- Use Natural Pressure Release for tougher cuts of meat, recipes with high starch (like rice or grains), and recipes with a high volume of liquid. This means you let the Instant Pot naturally release pressure. The little bobbin will fall once pressure is released completely.
- Use Quick Release for more delicate cuts of meat, such as seafood and chicken breasts, and for steaming vegetables. This means you manually turn the vent (being careful not to put your hand over the vent) to release the pressure. The little bobbin will fall once pressure is released completely.
- Make sure there is a clear pathway for the steam to release. The last thing you want is to ruin the bottom of your cupboards with all that steam.
- You *must* use liquid in the Instant Pot. The *minimum* amount of liquid you should have in the inner pot is ½ cup, but most recipes work best with at least 1 cup.
- Do *not* overfill the Instant Pot! It should only be ½ full for rice or beans (food that expands greatly when cooked) or ⅔ of the way full for almost everything else. Do not fill it to the max fill line.
- In this book, the cook time *does not* take into account the amount of time it will take the Instant Pot to come to pressure, or the amount of time it will take the Instant Pot to release pressure. Be aware of this when choosing a recipe to make.

- If the Instant Pot is not coming to pressure, it's usually because the sealing ring is not on properly, or the vent is not set to "sealing."
- The more liquid, or the colder the ingredients, the longer it will take for the Instant Pot to come to pressure.
- Always make sure that the Instant Pot is dry before inserting the inner pot, and make sure the inner pot is dry before inserting it into the Instant Pot.
- Use a binder clip to hold the inner pot tight against the outer pot when sautéing and stirring. This will keep the pot from "spinning" in the base.
- Doubling a recipe does not change the cook time, but instead it will take longer to come up to pressure.
- You do not always need to double the liquid when doubling a recipe. Depending on what you're making, more liquid may make the food too watery. Use your best judgment.
- When using the slow-cooker function, use the following chart:

Slow Cooker	Instant Pot
Warm	Less or Low
Low	Normal or Medium
High	More or High

Instant Pot Accessories

Most Instant Pots come with a stainless steel trivet. Below, you will find a list of common accessories that are frequently used in most Fix-It and Forget-It Instant Pot cookbooks. Most of these accessories can be purchased in-store or online.

- Steamer basket—stainless steel or silicone
- 7-inch nonstick or silicone springform or cake pan
- Sling or trivet with handles
- 1½-quart round baking dish
- Silicone egg molds

Soups, Stews & Chilis

Chicken & Turkey
Soups, Stews & Chilis

Black Bean Soup with Chicken and Salsa

Hope Comerford, Clinton Township, MI

Makes 4–6 Servings
Prep. Time: 10 minutes & Cooking Time: 6–8 hours & Ideal slow-cooker size: 5- to 6-qt.

4 cups chicken broth

1 large boneless, skinless chicken breast

2 (15-oz.) cans black beans, rinsed and drained

16-oz. jar salsa

1 cup frozen corn

1 cup sliced fresh mushrooms

½ red onion, chopped

1 Jalapeño pepper (whole)

1½ tsp. cumin

Salt to taste

Pepper to taste

Toppings:

Shredded cheese, *optional*

Sour cream, *optional*

Cilantro, *optional*

Avocado, *optional*

1. Place all ingredients except the toppings in the slow cooker. Stir.

2. Cover and cook on Low for 6–8 hours.

3. Remove the chicken and shred between two forks. Put it back in the soup and stir.

Variation:

You may chop up the jalapeño for extra heat. Leaving it whole provides the flavor without the heat.

Serving suggestion:

Serve garnished with the optional toppings.

Instant Pot Adaptation:

1. You can choose to sauté the meat first, or add it with all of the remaining ingredients except the toppings, just like you would in the slow cooker.

2. Secure the lid and set the vent to sealing. Set the Instant Pot to Soup and set for 10 minutes.

3. When cook time is over, manually release the pressure. When the pin drops, remove the lid and continue with step 3 above.

Chicken Noodle Soup

Colleen Heatwole, Burton, MI

Makes 6–8 servings
Prep. Time: 15 minutes & Cooking Time: 4 minutes

2 Tbsp. butter

1 Tbsp. oil

1 medium onion, diced

2 large carrots, diced

3 celery stalks, diced

Salt to taste

3 garlic cloves, minced

1 tsp. thyme

1 tsp. oregano

1 tsp. basil

8 cups chicken broth

2 cups cubed cooked chicken

8 oz. medium egg noodles

1 cup frozen peas (thaw while preparing soup)

Pepper to taste

1. In the inner pot of the Instant Pot, melt the butter with oil on the Sauté function.

2. Add onion, carrots, and celery with large pinch of salt and continue cooking on sauté until soft, about 5 minutes, stirring frequently.

3. Add garlic, thyme, oregano, and basil and sauté an additional minute.

4. Add broth, cooked chicken, and noodles, stirring to combine all ingredients.

5. Put lid on the Instant Pot and set vent to sealing. Select Manual high pressure and add 4 minutes.

6. When time is up do a quick (manual) release of the pressure.

7. Add thawed peas, stir, adjust seasoning with salt and pepper, and serve.

Slow-Cooker Adaptation:

1. (You may omit the butter or use it.) Add all the ingredients, except the egg noodles and frozen peas, to a 6-quart slow cooker.

2. Cover and cook on Low for 4 hours, or High for 2 hours.

3. Cook the egg noodles according to package instructions.

4. Add the frozen peas in the last 30 minutes or so.

5. To serve, portion the egg noodles into each bowl and spoon the broth over the top.

Note from the cook:

You can also prepare chicken for this recipe in the Instant Pot, but usually for this recipe, I use leftovers.

Chicken and Vegetable Soup

Hope Comerford, Clinton Township, MI

Makes 4–6 servings

Prep. Time: 15 minutes ⚜ *Cooking Time: 7–8 hours* ⚜ *Ideal slow-cooker size: 5-qt.*

I lb. boneless, skinless chicken, cut into bite-sized pieces

2 celery stalks, diced

I small yellow squash, diced

4 oz. mushrooms, sliced

2 large carrots, diced

I medium onion, chopped

2 Tbsp. garlic powder

I Tbsp. onion powder

I Tbsp. basil

½ tsp. no-salt seasoning

I tsp. salt

Pepper to taste

32 oz. low-sodium chicken stock

1. Place the chicken, vegetables, and spices into the crock. Pour the chicken stock over the top.

2. Cover and cook on Low for 7–8 hours, or until vegetables are tender.

Italiano Chicken, Rice, and Tomato Soup

Jane Geigley, Lancaster, PA

Makes 6 servings
Prep. Time: 30 minutes   ⚬   Cooking Time: 4–6 hours   ⚬   Ideal slow-cooker size: 4-qt.

½ cup chopped onion

2 Tbsp. butter, softened

½ tsp. paprika

½ tsp. basil

⅛ tsp. garlic powder

8-oz. brick cream cheese, softened

1¼ cups milk

2 (10¾-oz.) cans tomato soup

2 (16-oz.) cans whole tomatoes, undrained

1 cup instant rice

2 cups cooked chopped chicken

1 cup shredded mozzarella cheese

1. In a stand mixer, mix the first 9 ingredients. Beat until smooth. Pour into the slow cooker.

2. Stir in rice and chicken.

3. Cover and cook on Low for 4–6 hours. Add the shredded cheese at the very end, just before serving.

Chicken Tortilla Soup

Becky Fixel, Grosse Pointe Farms, MI

Makes 10–12 servings
Prep. Time: 5 minutes ⚘ *Cooking Time: 7–8 hours* ⚘ *Ideal slow-cooker size: 5-qt.*

2 lb. boneless, skinless chicken breast

32 oz. chicken stock

14 oz. salsa verde

10-oz. can diced tomatoes with lime juice

15-oz. can sweet corn, drained

1 Tbsp. minced garlic

1 small onion, diced

1 Tbsp. chili pepper

½ tsp. fresh ground pepper

½ tsp. salt

½ tsp. oregano

1 Tbsp. dried jalapeño slices

1. Add all ingredients to the slow cooker.

2. Cook on Low for 7–8 hours.

3. Approximately 30 minutes before the end, remove the chicken and shred it into small pieces.

Serving suggestion:

Top with a dollop of nonfat plain Greek yogurt, shredded cheese, fresh jalapeños, or fresh cilantro.

Instant Pot Adaptation:

1. You can choose to sauté the chicken first with some oil on the Sauté function, or skip this step and add it with all of the remaining ingredients into the inner pot.

2. Secure the lid, and set the vent to sealing. Set the Instant Pot to Soup and set for 10 minutes.

3. When cook time is over, manually release the pressure. When the pin drops, remove the lid.

4. Remove the chicken and shred it or cut it into small pieces, then place back in the soup.

Family Favorite Chicken Fajita Soup

Maria Shevlin, Sicklerville, NJ

Makes 10–12 servings
Prep. Time: 20 minutes & Cooking Time: 5 minutes

1 Tbsp. olive oil

1 medium onion, chopped

5 celery stalks, sliced down the center lengthwise, then chopped

4 garlic cloves, minced

1 cup frozen corn

5 cups chicken stock

2 cups water

32 oz. picante sauce (we love Pace)

¾ tsp. cumin

1 heaping Tbsp. chili powder

1 heaping Tbsp. paprika

½ cup celery leaves, chopped

4 cups precooked chicken (you can use a rotisserie chicken for this)

15-oz. can black beans, rinsed and drained

3 bell peppers, chopped

Toppings:

Green onion, chopped, *optional*

Tortilla strips, *optional*

Sour cream, *optional*

Mexican blend or taco seasoning, *optional*

Shredded cheese, *optional*

Sliced jalapeños, *optional*

1. Set the Instant Pot to the Sauté setting and let it get hot. Add the oil.

2. Sauté the onion, celery, and garlic for approximately 3–5 minutes.

3. Add the corn and mix well.

4. Stir in the chicken stock, water, picante sauce, and spices, including the celery leaves.

5. Add the precooked chicken, beans, and peppers, and mix well.

6. Secure the lid and set the vent to sealing. Manually set the cook time for 5 minutes on high pressure.

7. When cook time is up, manually release the pressure.

8. To serve, ladle into bowls and top with any, or all, of the optional toppings you want.

Quick Taco Chicken Soup

Karen Waggoner, Joplin, MO

Makes 4–6 servings
Prep Time: 5 minutes ⚜ Cooking Time: 1 hour ⚜ Ideal slow-cooker size: 4-qt.

12-oz. can cooked chicken, undrained
14-oz. can chicken broth
16-oz. jar mild thick-and-chunky salsa
15-oz. can ranch-style beans
15-oz. can whole-kernel corn

1. Mix all ingredients in the slow cooker.

2. Cover and cook on High for 1 hour. Keep warm on Low until ready to serve.

Instant Pot Adaptation:

1. Place all ingredients into the inner pot and secure the lid. Set the vent to sealing.
2. Set the cook time for 5 minutes on high pressure.
3. When the cook time is up, manually release the pressure. When the pin drops, remove the lid and serve.

Taco Soup

Marla Folkerts, Holland, OH

Makes 6 servings
Prep. Time: 20 minutes ⚜ *Cooking Time: 4–6 hours* ⚜ *Ideal slow-cooker size: 3½- or 4-qt.*

Soup:

1 lb. lean ground turkey or ground beef

1 medium onion, chopped

1 medium green bell pepper, chopped

1 envelope dry reduced-sodium taco seasoning

½ cup water

4 cups reduced-sodium vegetable juice

1 cup chunky salsa

Toppings:

¾ cup shredded lettuce

6 Tbsp. fresh tomato, chopped

6 Tbsp. cheddar cheese, shredded

¼ cup green onions or chives, chopped

¼ cup sour cream or plain yogurt

1. Brown meat with onion in nonstick skillet. Drain.

2. Combine all soup ingredients in the slow cooker.

3. Cover. Cook on Low for 4–6 hours.

4. Serve with your choice of toppings.

Instant Pot Adaptation:

1. Set the Instant Pot to Sauté. Heat up about 1 Tbsp. of oil of your choice and brown the ground meat. Remove the grease.

2. Pour in the ½ cup water and scrape the bottom of the pot. Add the remaining soup ingredients, plus an additional ¼ cup water.

3. Secure the lid and set the vent to sealing. Set the cook time on Soup for 10 minutes.

4. When cook time is up, manually release the pressure. When the pin drops, remove the lid and stir.

5. Serve with your choice of toppings.

Buffalo Chicken Wing Soup

SLOW COOKER

Mary Lynn Miller, Reinholds, PA
Donna Neiter, Wausau, WI
Joette Droz, Kalona, IA

Makes 8 servings
Prep. Time: 10 minutes & Cooking Time: 4–5 hours & Ideal slow-cooker size: 3-qt.

6 cups milk

3 (10¾-oz.) cans condensed cream of chicken soup, undiluted

3 cups (about 1 lb.) shredded or cubed cooked chicken

1 cup (8 oz.) sour cream

1–8 Tbsp. hot pepper sauce, according to your preference for heat

1. Combine milk and soup in the slow cooker until smooth.

2. Stir in chicken.

3. Cover and cook on Low for 3¾–4¾ hours.

4. Fifteen minutes before serving, stir in sour cream and hot sauce.

5. Cover and continue cooking just until bubbly.

White Chicken Chili

Judy Gascho, Woodburn, OR

Makes 6 servings
Prep. Time: 20 minutes ⚖ Cooking Time: 30 minutes

2 Tbsp. cooking oil

1½–2 lb. boneless chicken breasts or thighs

1 medium onion, chopped

3 garlic cloves, minced

2 cups chicken broth

3 (15-oz.) cans great northern beans, undrained

15-oz. can white corn, drained

4½-oz. can chopped green chilies, undrained

1 tsp. cumin

½ tsp. ground oregano

1 cup sour cream

1½ cups grated cheddar or Mexican blend cheese

Serving suggestion:
Can serve with chopped cilantro and additional cheese.

1. Set Instant Pot to Sauté and allow the inner pot to get hot.

2. Add oil and chicken. Brown chicken on both sides.

3. Add onion, garlic, chicken broth, undrained beans, drained corn, undrained green chilies, cumin, and oregano.

4. Place lid on and close valve to sealing.

5. Set to Bean/Chili for 30 minutes.

6. Let pressure release naturally for 15 minutes before carefully releasing any remaining steam.

7. Remove chicken and shred.

8. Put chicken, sour cream, and cheese in the inner pot. Stir until cheese is melted.

Slow-Cooker Adaptation:

1. Omit the oil. Place all ingredients, except the sour cream and grated cheese, into the crock of your slow-cooker (ideally a 5-qt. slow cooker).

2. Place the lid on the crock and cook on Low for 6 hours.

3. Remove the chicken and shred.

4. Put chicken, sour cream, and cheese in the crock. Stir until cheese is melted.

Chicken Chili

Sharon Miller, Holmesville, OH

Makes 6 servings
Prep. Time: 15 minutes ♣ Cooking Time: 5–6 hours ♣ Ideal slow-cooker size: 4-quart

2 lb. boneless, skinless chicken breasts, cubed

2 Tbsp. butter

2 (14-oz.) cans diced tomatoes, undrained

15-oz. can red kidney beans, rinsed and drained

1 cup diced onion

1 cup diced red bell pepper

1–2 Tbsp. chili powder, according to your taste preference

1 tsp. cumin

1 tsp. dried oregano

Salt to taste

Pepper to taste

1. In skillet on high heat, brown chicken cubes in butter until they have some browned edges. Place in greased slow cooker.

2. Pour one of the cans of tomatoes with its juice into skillet to get all the browned bits and butter. Scrape and pour into slow cooker.

3. Add rest of ingredients, including other can of tomatoes, to cooker.

4. Cook on Low for 5–6 hours.

Serving suggestion:

You can serve this chili with shredded cheddar cheese and sour cream.

Southwestern Chili

Colleen Heatwole, Burton, MI

Makes 12 servings
Prep. Time: 30 minutes ⚜ *Cooking Time: 6–8 hours* ⚜ *Ideal slow-cooker size: 6- or 7-qt.*

32-oz. can whole tomatoes

15-oz. jar salsa

15-oz. can low-sodium chicken broth

1 cup barley

3 cups water

1 tsp. chili powder

1 tsp. ground cumin

15-oz. can black beans

15-oz. can whole kernel corn

3 cups chopped cooked chicken

1 cup low-fat shredded cheddar cheese, *optional*

Low-fat sour cream, *optional*

1. Combine all ingredients in the slow cooker except for the cheese and sour cream.

2. Cover and cook on Low for 6–8 hours.

3. Serve with cheese and sour cream on each bowl, if desired.

Instant Pot Adaptation:

1. In the inner pot, add all the ingredients except for the cheese and sour cream.

2. Secure the lid and set the vent to sealing. Set the cook time for 18 minutes on high pressure.

3. When cook time is over, let the pressure release naturally for 10 minutes, then manually release the remaining pressure.

4. When the pin drops, remove the lid.

5. Serve with cheese and sour cream on each bowl, if desired.

Pork
Soups, Stews & Chilis

Shredded Pork Tortilla Soup

Hope Comerford, Clinton Township, MI

Makes 6–8 servings
Prep. Time: 10 minutes   ★   Cooking Time: 8–10 hours   ★   Ideal slow-cooker size: 5-quart

3 large tomatoes, chopped

1 cup chopped red onion

1 jalapeño, seeded and minced

1 lb. pork loin

2 tsp. cumin

2 tsp. chili powder

2 tsp. onion powder

2 tsp. garlic powder

2 tsp. lime juice

8 cups chicken broth

Garnishes:

Fresh chopped cilantro, *optional*

Tortilla chips, *optional*

Avocado slices, *optional*

Freshly grated Mexican cheese, *optional*

Tip:
If you don't have time for freshly chopped tomatoes, use a can of diced or chopped tomatoes.

1. In the crock, place the tomatoes, onion, and jalapeño.

2. Place the pork loin on top.

3. Add all the seasonings and lime juice, then pour in the chicken broth.

4. Cover and cook on Low for 8–10 hours.

5. Remove the pork and shred it between two forks. Place it back into the soup and stir.

6. Serve each bowl of soup with fresh chopped cilantro, tortilla chips, avocado slices, and freshly grated Mexican cheese, if desired . . . or any other garnishes you would like!

Instant Pot Adaptation:

1. Add all the ingredients to the inner pot, except for the garnishes.
2. Secure the lid and set the vent to sealing. Set the cook time for 70 minutes on high pressure.
3. When cook time is up, let the pressure release naturally for 10 minutes, then manually release any remaining pressure. When the pin drops, remove the lid.
4. Continue with steps 5 and 6 above.

Kielbasa Soup

Bernice M. Gnidovec, Streator, IL

Makes 8 servings
Prep. Time: 10 minutes ❧ Cooking Time: 12 hours ❧ Ideal slow-cooker size: 8-qt.

16-oz. pkg. frozen mixed vegetables, or
your choice of vegetables

6-oz. can tomato paste

1 medium onion, chopped

3 medium potatoes, diced

1½ lb. kielbasa, cut into ¼-inch pieces

4 qt. water

1. Combine all ingredients in large slow cooker.

2. Cover. Cook on Low for 12 hours.

Instant Pot Adaptation:

1. Set the Instant Pot to the Sauté function and heat up 1 Tbsp. oil of your choice.

2. Sauté the kielbasa and onion until browned.

3. Pour in ½ cup water and scrape any bits off the bottom of the inner pot.

4. Add the vegetables, tomato paste, and pour in water until you reach the fill line.

5. Secure the lid and set the vent to sealing. Set the cook time for 4 minutes on high pressure.

6. When cook time is up, let the pressure release naturally for 10 minutes, then manually release any remaining pressure. When the pin drops, remove the lid and serve.

Split Pea Soup

Judy Gascho, Woodburn, OR

Makes 3–4 servings
Prep. Time: 20 minutes ⚭ *Cooking Time: 15 minutes*

4 cups chicken broth

4 sprigs thyme

4 oz. ham, diced (about ⅓ cup)

2 Tbsp. butter

2 celery stalks

2 carrots

1 large leek

3 garlic cloves

1½ cups dried green split peas
(about 12 oz.)

Salt to taste

Pepper to taste

1. Pour the broth into the inner pot of the Instant Pot and set to Sauté. Add the thyme, ham, and butter.

2. While the broth heats, chop the celery and cut the carrots into ½-inch-thick rounds. Halve the leek lengthwise and thinly slice and chop the garlic. Add the vegetables to the pot as you cut them. Rinse the split peas in a colander, discarding any small stones, then add to the pot.

3. Secure the lid, making sure the steam valve is in the sealing position. Set the cooker to Manual at high pressure for 15 minutes. When the time is up, carefully turn the steam valve to the venting position to release the pressure manually.

4. Turn off the Instant Pot. Remove the lid and stir the soup; discard the thyme sprigs.

5. Thin the soup with up to 1 cup water if needed (the soup will continue to thicken as it cools). Season with salt and pepper.

Slow-Cooker Adaptation:

1. Rinse the split peas and discard any stones, then place them into a 6-quart or larger slow cooker. Add all the remaining ingredients, except the butter which can be omitted.

2. Place the lid on the crock and cook on Low for 8 hours. Remove the lid and stir the soup; discard the thyme sprigs.

3. Continue at step 5 above.

INSTANT POT

Potato Bacon Soup

Colleen Heatwole, Burton, MI

Makes 4–6 servings
Prep. Time: 30 minutes ⚭ Cooking Time: 5 minutes

5 lb. potatoes, peeled and cubed

3 celery stalks, diced into ¼- to ½-inch pieces

1 large onion, chopped

1 clove garlic, minced

1 Tbsp. seasoning salt

½ tsp. pepper

4 cups chicken broth

1 lb. bacon, fried crisp and rough chopped

1 cup half-and-half

1 cup milk, 2% or whole

Garnishes:

Sour cream, *optional*

Shredded cheddar cheese, *optional*

Diced green onion, *optional*

1. Place potatoes in bottom of the Instant Pot inner pot.

2. Add celery, onion, garlic, seasoning salt, and pepper, then stir to combine.

3. Add chicken broth and bacon to pot and stir to combine.

4. Secure the lid and make sure vent is in the sealing position. Using Manual mode select 5 minutes, high pressure.

5. Manually release the pressure when cooking time is up. Open pot and mash potatoes, leaving some large chunks if desired.

6. Add half-and-half and milk.

7. Serve while still hot with desired assortment of garnishes.

Notes:

• I like this recipe because it requires no sautéing of onion, garlic, or celery but still tastes good.

• I have used a variety of potatoes for this recipe. We raise mostly Kennebec but also red potatoes. My spouse likes this recipe with either.

Sausage and Kale Chowder

Beverly Hummel, Fleetwood, PA

Makes 6 servings
Prep. Time: 20 minutes ❧ Cooking Time: 5 hours ❧ Ideal slow-cooker size: 4- to 5-qt.

I lb. bulk sausage
I cup chopped onion
6 small red potatoes, chopped
I cup thinly sliced kale, ribs removed
6 cups chicken broth
I cup milk, at room temperature
Salt
Pepper

1. Brown sausage. Drain off grease. Transfer sausage to slow cooker.

2. Add onion, potatoes, kale, and broth.

3. Cook on High for 4 hours, until potatoes and kale are soft.

4. Add milk and cook on Low for 1 hour. Season to taste with salt and black pepper.

Serving suggestion:

Italian bread and salad make a great accompaniment to this chowder.

Tip:

If you prefer a thicker soup, add 2 tablespoons cornstarch to milk in Step 4 before adding to cooker. Stir several times in the last hour as chowder thickens.

Beef
Soups, Stews & Chilis

Stuffed Sweet Pepper Soup

Moreen Weaver, Bath, NY

Makes 10 servings
Prep. Time: 20 minutes ⚬ Cooking Time: 6 hours ⚬ Ideal slow-cooker size: 6-qt.

1 lb. 95%-lean ground beef

2 qt. low-sodium tomato juice

3 medium red, or green, bell peppers, diced

1½ cups no-salt-added chili sauce

2 celery stalks, diced

1 large onion, diced

3 low-sodium chicken bouillon cubes

2 garlic cloves, minced

1 cup uncooked brown rice, prepared according to package instructions

Tip:

To make this recipe vegetarian and/or plant-based, replace the ground beef with meatless crumbles, or use beans instead and replace the chicken bouillon cubes with vegetable bouillon cubes.

1. In skillet over medium heat, cook beef until no longer pink. Drain off drippings.

2. Add the browned beef to the slow-cooker insert along with all the remaining ingredients.

3. Place the lid on the slow cooker and set on Low for 6 hours.

4. Just before the end of the cook time, cook the brown rice.

5. To serve, place a bit of rice in each bowl, then spoon the soup over the top.

Instant Pot Adaptation:

1. Set the Instant Pot to the Sauté function. Add the ground beef and sauté until browned. Drain the grease.

2. Add ½ cup of the 2 quarts of tomato juice to the inner pot and scrape the bottom of the pot to take off any browned bits.

3. Add the rest of the tomato juice, peppers, chili sauce, celery, onion, bouillon cubes, and garlic. Pour the rice on top, but *do not stir.* Just press it down so it is under the liquid.

4. Secure the lid and set the vent to sealing. Set the cook time for 5 minutes on high pressure.

5. When cook time is over, let the pressure release naturally for 5 minutes, then manually release the remaining pressure. When the pin drops, remove the lid and serve.

Unstuffed Cabbage Soup

Colleen Heatwole, Burton, MI

Makes 4–6 servings
Prep. Time: 15 minutes ♣ Cooking Time: 10–20 minutes

2 Tbsp. coconut oil

1 lb. ground beef, turkey, or venison

1 medium onion, diced

2 garlic cloves, minced

1 small head cabbage, chopped, cored, cut into 2-inch pieces.

6-oz. can tomato paste

32-oz. can diced tomatoes, with liquid

2 cups beef broth

1½ cups water

¾ cup white or brown rice

1–2 tsp. salt

½ tsp. pepper

1 tsp. oregano

1 tsp. parsley

1. Melt coconut oil in the inner pot of the Instant Pot using Sauté function. Add ground meat. Stir frequently until meat loses color, about 2 minutes.

2. Add onion and garlic and continue to sauté for 2 more minutes, stirring frequently.

3. Add chopped cabbage.

4. On top of cabbage layer tomato paste, tomatoes with liquid, beef broth, water, rice, and spices.

5. Secure the lid and set vent to sealing. Using Manual setting, select 10 minutes if using white rice, 20 minutes if using brown rice.

6. When time is up, let the pressure release naturally for 10 minutes, then do a quick release.

Slow-Cooker Adaptation:

1. On the stove, brown the ground meat of choice with the coconut oil, or omit the oil. Drain the grease.

2. Add all the remaining ingredients except the rice into a 6- to 8-qt. crock.

3. Place the lid on the crock and cook on Low for 8 hours.

4. When it's close to the end of cook time, prepare the rice according to the package instructions.

5. When serving, place a bit of rice in each bowl and spoon the soup over the top.

Slow-Cooker Beef Stew

Becky Fixel, Grosse Pointe Farms, MI

Makes 8–10 servings
Prep. Time: 30 minutes ⚬ Cooking Time: 6 hours ⚬ Ideal slow-cooker size: 3-qt.

2 lb. stew beef, cubed
¼ cup white rice flour
1½ tsp. salt
½ tsp. pepper
32 oz. beef broth
1 onion, diced
1 tsp. Worcestershire sauce
1 bay leaf
1 tsp. paprika
4 carrots, sliced
3 potatoes, sliced thinly
1 celery stalk, sliced

1. Place the meat in crock.

2. Mix the flour, salt, and pepper. Pour over the meat and mix well. Make sure to cover the meat with flour.

3. Add broth to the crock and stir well.

4. Add remaining ingredients and stir to mix well.

5. Cook on High for at least 5 hours, then on Low for 1 hour. Remove bay leaf and serve.

Instantly Good Beef Stew

Hope Comerford, Clinton Township, MI

Makes 6 servings
Prep. Time: 20 minutes & Cooking Time: 35 minutes

3 Tbsp. olive oil, *divided*

2 lb. stewing beef, cubed

2 garlic cloves, minced

1 large onion, chopped

3 celery stalks, sliced

3 large potatoes, cubed

2–3 carrots, sliced

8 oz. no-salt-added tomato sauce

10 oz. low-sodium beef broth

2 tsp. Worcestershire sauce

¼ tsp. pepper

1 bay leaf

1. Set the Instant Pot to the Sauté function, then add 1 tablespoon of the oil. Add ⅓ of the beef cubes and brown and sear all sides. Repeat this process twice more with the remaining oil and beef cubes. Set the beef aside.

2. Place the garlic, onion, and celery into the pot and sauté for a few minutes. Press Cancel.

3. Add the beef back in as well as all the remaining ingredients.

4. Secure the lid and make sure the vent is set to sealing. Choose Manual for 35 minutes.

5. When the cook time is over, let the pressure release naturally for 15 minutes, then release any remaining pressure manually.

6. Remove the lid, remove the bay leaf, then serve.

Note:

If you want the stew to be a bit thicker, remove some of the potatoes, mash, then stir them back through the stew.

Tuscan Beef Stew

Orpha Herr, Andover, NY

Makes 12 servings
Prep. Time: 20 minutes   ♨   Cooking Time: 8–9 hours   ♨   Ideal slow-cooker size: 6-qt.

10¾-oz. can tomato soup

1½ cups beef broth

½ cup burgundy or other red wine

1 tsp. Italian herb seasoning

½ tsp. garlic powder

14½-oz. can diced Italian-style tomatoes, undrained

½ cup diced onion

3 large carrots, cut in 1-inch pieces

2 lb. stew beef, cut into 1-inch pieces

2 (16-oz.) cans cannellini beans, rinsed and drained

1. Stir soup, broth, wine, Italian seasoning, garlic powder, tomatoes, onion, carrots, and beef into slow cooker.

2. Cover and cook on Low for 8–9 hours or until vegetables are tender-crisp.

3. Stir in beans. Turn to High until heated through, 10–20 minutes more.

Meme's Meatball Stew

Maxine Phaneuf, Washington, MI

Makes 6–8 servings
Prep Time: 10 minutes ⚶ *Cooking Time: 15 minutes*

Meatballs:

1½ lb. lean ground beef

1-oz. pkg. onion soup mix

¾ cup Italian bread crumbs

1 egg

Stew:

7 cups water

11¾-oz. can condensed tomato soup

2½ carrots, peeled and chopped

2 potatoes, peeled and chopped

2 big handfuls fresh green beans, chopped

1 medium onion, chopped

1–2 tsp. salt

½ tsp. pepper

2 tsp. onion powder

2 tsp. garlic powder

Note:

You can use tomato sauce in place of the condensed tomato soup.

1. In a medium bowl, mix the meatball ingredients and form into golf ball–size meatballs.

2. In the inner pot of the Instant Pot, add the stew ingredients. Carefully drop in the meatballs.

3. Secure the lid and set the vent to sealing. Manually set the cook time for 15 minutes on high pressure.

4. When the cook time is over, let the pressure release naturally for 10 minutes, then manually release the remaining pressure.

Serving suggestion:

Serve each bowl with grated Parmesan cheese and a side of crusty Italian bread with butter.

Slow-Cooker Adaptation:

1. In a medium bowl, mix the meatball ingredients and form into golf ball–size meatballs.

2. Brown the meatballs in small batches in a pan on the stove with a bit of oil of your choice.

3. Add all the remaining ingredients into the crock of your slow-cooker (ideally an 8-qt. slow cooker), then place the meatballs into the liquid.

4. Place the lid on the crock and cook on Low for 7–9 hours.

Our Favorite Chili

Ruth Shank, Gridley, IL

Makes 10–12 servings
Prep. Time: 20 minutes ⚘ Cooking Time: 4–10 hours ⚘ Ideal slow-cooker size: 5-qt.

1½ lb. extra-lean ground beef

¼ cup chopped onions

1 celery stalk, chopped

Extra-virgin olive oil, *optional*

29-oz. can stewed tomatoes

2 (15½-oz.) cans red kidney beans, drained, rinsed

2 (16-oz.) cans chili beans, undrained

½ cup ketchup

1½ tsp. lemon juice

2 tsp. vinegar

1 tsp. brown sugar

1½ tsp. kosher salt

1 tsp. Worcestershire sauce

½ tsp. garlic powder

½ tsp. dry mustard powder

1 Tbsp. chili powder

2 (6-oz.) cans tomato paste

1. Brown ground beef, onions, and celery in oil (if using) in skillet. Stir frequently to break up clumps of meat. When meat is no longer pink, drain off drippings.

2. Place meat and vegetables in the slow cooker. Add all remaining ingredients. Mix well.

3. Cover. Cook on Low for 8–10 hours or on High for 4–5 hours.

Chili Comerford Style

Hope Comerford, Clinton Township, MI

Makes 4–6 servings
Prep. Time:10 minutes ⚶ Cooking Time: 15 minutes

1 tsp. olive oil

1 lb. ground beef

1 medium onion, chopped

15½-oz. can kidney beans, rinsed and drained

2 (14½-oz.) cans diced tomatoes

10-oz. can cream of tomato soup (I use Pacific brand)

3 garlic cloves, minced

2 tsp. tarragon

1 tsp. salt

1 tsp. pepper

2 tsp. chili powder

1 cup beef stock

3–6 cups water, depending on how thick or thin you like your chili

1. Set the Instant Pot to the Sauté function and let it get hot. Pour in the olive oil and coat the bottom of the pot.

2. Brown the ground beef with the onion. This will take about 5–7 minutes.

3. Press Cancel. Carefully drain the grease.

4. Place the remaining ingredients into the inner pot with the beef and onion.

5. Secure the lid and set the vent to sealing. Manually set the cook time for 15 minutes on high pressure.

6. When cook time is up, manually release the pressure. When the pin drops, remove the lid and serve.

Serving suggestion:

We love to add a dollop of sour cream and a bit of shredded sharp cheddar to our chili.

Meatless
Soups, Stews & Chilis

Broccoli Cheese Soup

SLOW COOKER

Hope Comerford, Clinton Township, MI

Makes 6 servings
Prep. Time: 15 minutes ⚘ Cooking Time: 6–7 hours ⚘ Ideal slow-cooker size: 3-qt.

1 head broccoli, chopped into tiny pieces

1 onion, chopped finely

2 (12-oz.) cans evaporated milk

10¾-oz. can condensed cheddar cheese soup

3 cups water

4 vegetable bouillon cubes

1½ tsp. garlic powder

1 tsp. onion powder

½ tsp. seasoned salt

1 tsp. pepper

16-oz. block Velveeta cheese, chopped into pieces

1. Place all ingredients into crock, except for the Velveeta cheese, and stir.

2. Cover and cook on Low for 6–7 hours.

3. About 5–10 minutes before eating, turn slow cooker to High and stir in Velveeta cheese until melted.

Slow-Cooker Loaded Baked Potato Soup

Becky Fixel, Grosse Pointe Farms, MI

Makes 8–10 servings
Prep. Time: 15 minutes ⚜ Cooking Time: 6 hours ⚜ Ideal slow-cooker size: 5-qt.

32 oz. vegetable broth

2 cups heavy cream

5–7 medium potatoes, cubed

1 small onion, chopped

1. Empty the broth and cream into the crock.

2. Add the chopped potatoes and onion. Stir until combined.

3. Cover and cook on High for 6 hours.

4. With an immersion blender or a potato masher, mash any remaining chunks in the soup.

Serving suggestion:

Top with shredded cheese, cooked chopped bacon, and chopped green onions.

Creamy Wild Rice Mushroom Soup

INSTANT POT

Hope Comerford, Clinton Township, MI

Makes 4–6 servings
Prep. Time: 10 minutes ⚬ Cooking Time: 40 minutes

½ large onion, chopped

3 garlic cloves, chopped

3 celery stalks, chopped

3 carrots, chopped

8 oz. fresh baby bella mushrooms, sliced

I cup wild rice

4 cups low-sodium vegetable stock

½ tsp. dried thyme

¼ tsp. pepper

I cup fat-free half-and-half, heated

2 Tbsp. cornstarch

2 Tbsp. cold water

1. Place the onion, garlic, celery, carrots, mushrooms, wild rice, stock, thyme, and pepper in the inner pot of the Instant Pot and secure the lid. Make sure the vent is set to sealing.

2. Manually set the time for 30 minutes on high pressure.

3. When the cook time is over, manually release the pressure and remove the lid when the pin drops.

4. While the pressure is releasing, heat the half-in-half either in the microwave or on the stovetop.

5. Whisk together the cornstarch and cold water. Whisk this into the heated half-and-half.

6. Slowly whisk the half-and-half/cornstarch mixture into the soup in the Instant Pot. Serve and enjoy!

Minestrone

Bernita Boyts, Shawnee Mission, KS

Makes 8–10 servings
Prep. Time: 15 minutes ❧ Cooking Time: 4–9 hours ❧ Ideal slow-cooker size: 3½- to 4-qt.

1 large onion, chopped

4 carrots, sliced

3 celery stalks, sliced

2 garlic cloves, minced

1 Tbsp. olive oil

6-oz. can tomato paste

2 cups low-sodium vegetable broth

24-oz. can pinto beans, drained, rinsed

10-oz. pkg. frozen green beans

2–3 cups chopped cabbage

1 medium zucchini, sliced

8 cups water

2 Tbsp. parsley

2 Tbsp. Italian seasoning

1 tsp. sea salt, or more to taste

½ tsp. pepper

¾ cup dry acini di pepe (small round pasta)

Grated Parmesan or Asiago cheese, *optional*

1. Sauté onion, carrots, celery, and garlic in oil in skillet until tender. Add to slow cooker.

2. Combine all other ingredients, except pasta and cheese, in the slow cooker.

3. Cover. Cook 4–5 hours on High or 8–9 hours on Low.

4. Add pasta 1 hour before cooking is complete.

5. Top individual servings with cheese, if desired.

Instant Pot Adaptation:

1. Set the Instant Pot to the Sauté function. Sauté onion, carrots, celery, and garlic in the oil until tender.

2. Add the remaining ingredients, except the grated cheese. Make sure the pasta is under the liquid.

3. Secure the lid and set the vent to sealing. Set the cook time on the Soup function for 5 minutes.

4. When cook time is up, let the pressure release naturally for 5 minutes, then manually release the remaining pressure. When the pin drops, remove the lid.

5. Top individual servings with cheese, if desired.

Veggie Minestrone

Dorothy VanDeest, Memphis, TN

Makes 8 servings
Prep. Time: 5 minutes   Cooking Time: 4 minutes

2 Tbsp. olive oil

1 large onion, chopped

1 garlic clove, minced

4 cups low-sodium vegetable stock

16-oz. can kidney beans, rinsed and drained

14½-oz. can no-salt-added diced tomatoes

2 medium carrots, sliced thin

¼ tsp. dried oregano

¼ tsp. pepper

½ cup whole wheat elbow macaroni, uncooked

4 oz. fresh spinach

1. Set the Instant Pot to the Sauté function and heat the olive oil.

2. When the olive oil is heated, add the onion and garlic to the inner pot and sauté for 5 minutes.

3. Press Cancel and add the stock, kidney beans, tomatoes, carrots, oregano, and pepper. Gently pour in the macaroni, but *do not stir*. Just push the noodles gently under the liquid.

4. Secure the lid and set the vent to sealing.

5. Manually set the cook time for 4 minutes on high pressure.

6. When the cooking time is over, manually release the pressure and remove the lid when the pin drops.

7. Stir in the spinach and let wilt a few minutes before serving.

Enchilada Soup

Melissa Paskvan, Novi, MI

Makes 6–8 servings
Prep. Time: 5 minutes ⚹ Cooking Time: 6–8 hours ⚹ Ideal slow-cooker size: 6-qt.

14½-oz. can diced tomatoes with green chilies or chipotle

12-oz. jar enchilada sauce

4 cups vegetable broth

1 small onion, chopped

3 cups sliced tricolor bell peppers

10-oz. pkg. frozen corn

1 cup water

½ cup uncooked quinoa

1. Add all ingredients to slow cooker.

2. Cover and cook on Low for 6–8 hours.

Flavorful Tomato Soup

Shari Ladd, Hudson, MI

Makes 4 servings
Prep. Time: 10 minutes ⚖ *Cooking Time: 5 minutes*

1 Tbsp. extra-virgin olive oil

2 Tbsp. chopped onion

1 qt. no-salt-added stewed tomatoes

2 tsp. turbinado sugar or sugar substitute of your choice

½ tsp. pepper

¼ tsp. dried basil

½ tsp. dried oregano

¼ tsp. dried thyme

6 Tbsp. margarine

3 Tbsp. flour

2 cups skim milk

1. Set the Instant Pot to Sauté and heat the olive oil.

2. Sauté the onion for 5 minutes in the heated oil in the inner pot.

3. Press Cancel and add the tomatoes, sugar, pepper, basil, oregano, and thyme.

4. Secure the lid and set the vent to sealing.

5. Manually set the cook time for 5 minutes on high pressure.

6. When the cooking time is over, let the pressure release naturally for 15 minutes, then manually release the remaining pressure.

7. While the pressure is releasing, in a small pot on the stove, melt the margarine. Once the margarine is melted, whisk in the flour and cook for 2 minutes, whisking constantly.

8. Slowly whisk the skim milk into the pot.

9. When the pin has dropped next to the pressure valve, remove the lid and slowly whisk the milk/margarine/flour mixture into the tomato soup.

10. Use an immersion blender to puree the soup. Serve and enjoy!

Pasta Dishes

Chicken & Turkey
Pasta Dishes

Buffalo Chicken Pasta

Hope Comerford, Clinton Township, MI

Makes 8 servings
Prep. Time: 10 minutes   ❧   Cooking Time: 6 hours   ❧   Ideal slow-cooker size: 4- or 5-qt.

2 (10½-oz.) cans cream of chicken soup (I use Pacific brand)

¾ cup Buffalo wing sauce

1 medium red onion, finely chopped

1 tsp. garlic powder

¼ tsp. salt

2 lb. boneless, skinless chicken breast, chopped

1 lb. penne pasta, cooked according to pkg. instructions

2 cups sour cream

½ cup ranch dressing

1 cup mozzarella cheese

1. In the crock, mix the cream of chicken soup, Buffalo wing sauce, onion, garlic powder, and salt. Add the chicken pieces and stir again, coating them well.

2. Place the cover on the crock and cook on Low for 6 hours.

3. About a half hour before cook time is up, start the pasta so it's ready for you.

4. When cook time is over, mix the sour cream, ranch dressing, and mozzarella into the crock, then pour in the cooked pasta, coating everything well.

5. Serve and enjoy!

SLOW
COOKER

Turkey Slow-Cooker Pizza

Evelyn L. Ward, Greeley, CO
Ann Van Doren, Lady Lake, FL

Makes 8 servings
Prep. Time: 25 minutes ⚜ *Cooking Time: 3 hours* ⚜ *Ideal slow-cooker size: 6-qt.*

1½ lb. 99% lean ground turkey

¼ cup chopped onions

1 Tbsp. olive oil

28-oz. jar fat-free low-sodium spaghetti sauce

4½-oz. can sliced mushrooms, drained

1–1½ tsp. Italian seasoning, according to your taste preference

12-oz. pkg. wide egg noodles, slightly undercooked

2 cups fat-free shredded mozzarella cheese

2 cups low-fat, low-sodium shredded cheddar cheese

1. In a large skillet, cook turkey and onions in olive oil until turkey is no longer pink. Drain.

2. Stir in spaghetti sauce, mushrooms, and Italian seasoning.

3. Spray slow cooker with nonfat cooking spray. Spread ¼ of meat sauce in pot.

4. Cover with ⅓ of noodles. Top with ⅓ of cheeses.

5. Repeat layers twice.

6. Cover. Cook on Low for 3 hours. Do not overcook.

Tip:

You may create your own Italian seasoning by combining equal parts dried basil, oregano, rosemary, marjoram, thyme, and sage. Mix well. Stir in a tightly covered jar in a dry and dark place.

Chicken Italiano

Mary C. Casey, Scranton, PA

Makes 6 servings
Prep. Time: 15–20 minutes ♣ Cooking Time: 3½–6 hours ♣ Ideal slow-cooker size: 4-qt.

2 large whole boneless, skinless chicken breasts, each cut in 3 pieces

¾ tsp. salt

¼ tsp. pepper

½ tsp. dried oregano

½ tsp. dried basil

2 bay leaves

26-oz. jar marinara sauce

6 servings cooked pasta

1. Place chicken in bottom of slow cooker.

2. Sprinkle seasonings over chicken.

3. Pour sauce over seasoned meat, stirring to be sure chicken is completely covered.

4. Cover. Cook on Low for 6 hours or on High for 3½–4 hours.

6. Serve over pasta.

Instant Pot Adaptation:

1. In the inner pot of the Instant Pot, pour the marinara sauce and spices. Place the chicken on top.

2. Secure the lid and set the vent to sealing. Set the cook time for 15 minutes on high pressure. When cook time is up, manually release the pressure.

3. Serve over pasta.

Ground Turkey Cacciatore Spaghetti

Maria Shevlin, Sicklerville, NJ

Makes 6 servings
Prep. Time: 15–20 minutes ⚬ Cooking Time: 5 minutes

I tsp. olive oil

I medium sweet onion, chopped

3 garlic cloves, minced

I lb. ground turkey

32-oz. jar spaghetti sauce, or I qt. homemade

I tsp. salt

½ tsp. pepper

½ tsp. oregano

½ tsp. dried basil

½ tsp. red pepper flakes

I cup bell pepper strips, mixed colors if desired

I cup diced mushrooms

13¼-oz. box Dreamfield spaghetti

3 cups chicken bone broth

1. Press the Sauté button on the Instant Pot and add the oil, onion, and garlic to the inner pot.

2. Add the ground turkey and break it up a little while it browns.

3. Once ground turkey is browned, add the sauce and seasonings.

4. Add the bell peppers and mushrooms and give it a stir to mix.

5. Break the spaghetti noodles in half, then add them.

6. Add the chicken bone broth. Make sure the noodles are pushed under the liquid.

7. Lock lid, make sure the vent is at sealing, and set on Manual at high pressure for 6 minutes.

8. When cook time is up, manually release the pressure.

Serving suggestion:
Top with some fresh grated Parmesan cheese and basil.

Beef
Pasta Dishes

Beef Stroganoff

Gloria Julien, Gladstone, MI

Makes 6 servings
Prep. Time: 15 minutes & Cooking Time: 3½–4½ hours & Ideal slow-cooker size: 4-qt.

1½ lb. lean beef stewing meat, trimmed of fat

1 onion, chopped

1 clove garlic, minced

1 tsp. salt

¼ tsp. pepper

1 lb. fresh mushrooms

10¾-oz. can cream of mushroom soup

1 cup water

1 cup sour cream

1. Combine all ingredients except sour cream in the slow cooker.

2. Cook on Low for 3–4 hours.

3. Stir in sour cream.

4. Cook on High for a few minutes to heat sour cream.

Serving suggestion:
Serve over cooked egg noodles or cooked rice.

Steak Stroganoff

Marie Morucci, Glen Lyon, PA

Makes 6 servings
Prep. Time: 15 minutes & Cooking Time: 30 minutes

1 Tbsp. olive oil

2 Tbsp. flour

½ tsp. garlic powder

½ tsp. pepper

¼ tsp. paprika

1¾-pound boneless beef round steak, trimmed of fat, cut into 1½ × ½-inch strips

10¾-oz. can reduced-sodium, 98% fat-free cream of mushroom soup

½ cup water

1 envelope sodium-free dried onion soup mix

9-oz. jar sliced mushrooms, drained

½ cup fat-free sour cream

1 tablespoon minced fresh parsley

1. Place the oil in the inner pot of the Instant Pot and press Sauté.

2. Combine flour, garlic powder, pepper, and paprika in a small bowl. Stir the steak pieces through the flour mixture until they are evenly coated.

3. Lightly brown the steak pieces in the oil in the Instant Pot, about 2 minutes each side. Press Cancel when done.

4. Stir the mushroom soup, water, and onion soup mix, then pour over the steak.

5. Secure the lid and set the vent to sealing. Press the Manual button and set for 15 minutes.

6. When cook time is up, let the pressure release naturally for 15 minutes, then release the rest manually.

7. Remove the lid and press Cancel, then Sauté. Stir in mushrooms, sour cream, and parsley. Let the sauce come to a boil and cook for about 10–15 minutes.

Slow-Cooker Adaptation:

1. Combine flour, garlic powder, pepper, and paprika in a 4-quart slow cooker.
2. Cut meat into 1½ × ½-inch strips. Place in flour mixture and toss until meat is well coated.
3. Add mushroom soup, water, and soup mix. Stir until well blended.
4. Cover. Cook on High for 3–3½ hours or on Low for 6–7 hours.
5. Stir in mushrooms, sour cream, and parsley. Cover and cook on High for 10–15 minutes, or until heated through.

Beef in Noodles

Hope Comerford, Clinton Township, MI

Makes 4–6 servings
Prep. Time: 10 minutes ⚸ Cooking Time: 38–40 minutes

4 Tbsp. butter
1 ½ lb. stew beef
½ tsp. salt
¼ tsp. pepper
6 cups beef broth, *divided*
1 tsp. garlic power
1 tsp. onion powder
1 Tbsp. Worcestershire sauce
1 tsp. low-sodium soy sauce
½ cup cornstarch
½ cup cold water
24 oz. egg noodles

1. Set the Instant Pot to the Sauté function and let it get hot.

2. Melt the butter, then immediately add the beef, season with the salt and pepper, and brown on all sides.

3. Add 1 cup of the broth and deglaze the pot, scraping up any stuck-on bits. Press Cancel.

4. Add the remaining broth, garlic powder, onion powder, Worcestershire sauce, and soy sauce.

5. Secure the lid and set the vent to sealing. Manually set the cook time for 28 minutes on high pressure.

6. When cook time is up, manually release the pressure.

7. When the pin drops, remove the lid. In a small bowl, mix the cornstarch and water, then add it to the pot, stirring.

8. Stir in the egg noodles and switch the Instant Pot to the Sauté function once again. Place the lid on the pot and allow the noodles to simmer for 6–8 minutes, or until tender.

Cheese Tortellini and Meatballs with Vodka Pasta Sauce

Phyllis Good, Lancaster, PA

Makes 4–6 servings

Prep. Time: 10 minutes ❧ *Cooking Time: 6 hours* ❧ *Ideal slow-cooker size: 5-qt.*

1½-lb. bag frozen cheese tortellini
1½-lb. bag frozen Italian-style meatballs
20-oz. jar vodka pasta sauce
8-oz. can tomato sauce
1 cup water
½ tsp. red pepper flakes, or less if you want
1½ tsp. dried oregano
1½ tsp. dried basil
2 cups grated mozzarella cheese

1. Combine all ingredients except cheese in a greased slow cooker.

2. Cook on Low for 6 hours.

3. Top each serving with grated cheese.

Instant Pot Adaptation:

1. Place all ingredients except cheese in the inner pot of the Instant Pot. Add an additional ¼ cup water. *Do not stir.*

2. Secure the lid and set the vent to sealing. Set the cook time for 8 minutes on high pressure.

3. When cook time is up, manually release the pressure. When the pin drops, remove the lid. This will thicken as it sits with the lid off.

4. Top each serving with grated cheese.

Convenient Slow-Cooker Lasagna

Rachel Yoder, Middlebury, IN

Makes 6–8 servings
Prep. Time: 30–45 minutes   ♣   Cooking Time: 4 hours   ♣   Ideal slow-cooker size: 6-qt.

1 lb. extra-lean ground beef

29-oz. can tomato sauce

8-oz. pkg. lasagna noodles, uncooked, *divided*

4 cups shredded low-fat mozzarella cheese

1½ cups low-fat cottage cheese

1. Spray the interior of the cooker with nonstick spray.

2. Brown the ground beef in a large nonstick skillet. Drain off drippings.

3. Stir in tomato sauce. Mix well.

4. Spread ¼ of the meat sauce on the bottom of the slow cooker.

5. Arrange ⅓ of the uncooked noodles over the sauce. If you wish, break them up so they fit better.

6. Combine the cheeses in a bowl. Spoon ⅓ of the cheeses over the noodles.

7. Repeat these layers twice.

8. Top with remaining meat sauce.

9. Cover and cook on Low for 4 hours.

Lasagna the Instant Pot Way

INSTANT POT

Hope Comerford, Clinton Township, MI

Makes 8 servings
Prep. Time: 15 minutes ⚘ Cooking Time: 15 minutes

1 Tbsp. olive oil

1 lb. extra-lean ground beef or ground turkey

½ cup chopped onion

½ tsp. salt

⅛ tsp. pepper

2 cups water

12 lasagna noodles

8 oz. cottage cheese

1 egg

1 tsp. Italian seasoning

4 cups spinach, chopped or torn

1 cup sliced mushrooms

28 oz. marinara sauce

1 cup mozzarella cheese

1. Set the Instant Pot to the Sauté function and heat the olive oil. Brown the beef and onion with the salt and pepper. This will take about 5 minutes. Because you're using extra-lean ground beef, there should not be much grease, but if so, you'll need to drain it before continuing. Remove half of the ground beef and set aside. Press Cancel.

2. Pour in the water.

3. Break 4 noodles in half and arrange them on top of the beef and water.

4. Mix together the cottage cheese, egg, and Italian seasoning until the mixture is smooth. Smooth half of this mixture over the lasagna noodles.

5. Layer half of the spinach and half of the mushrooms on top.

6. Break 4 more noodles in half and lay them on top of what you just did. Spread out the remaining cottage cheese mixture.

7. Layer on the remaining spinach and mushrooms, then pour half of the marinara sauce over the top.

8. Finish with breaking the remaining 4 noodles in half and laying them on top of the previous layer. Spread the remaining marinara sauce on top.

9. Secure the lid and set the vent to sealing. Manually set the cook time for 7 minutes on high pressure.

10. When the cook time is over, let the pressure release naturally for 10 minutes, then manually release the remaining pressure.

11. When the pin drops, remove the lid and sprinkle the mozzarella cheese on top. Re-cover for 5 minutes.

12. When the 5 minutes are up, remove the lid. You can let this sit for a while to thicken up on Keep Warm.

Meatless & Seafood Pasta Dishes

Macaroni and Cheese

Hope Comerford, Clinton Township, MI

Makes 8 servings
Prep. Time: 5 minutes ⚶ Cooking Time: 4 minutes

1 lb. uncooked elbow macaroni

2 cups water

2 cups vegetable broth

4 Tbsp. butter

1 tsp. salt

¼ tsp. pepper

1 tsp. hot sauce

1 tsp. mustard powder

½–1 cup heavy cream or milk

1 cup shredded Gouda cheese

1 cup shredded sharp cheddar cheese

1 cup shredded Monterey Jack cheese

1. Place the macaroni, water, broth, butter, salt, pepper, hot sauce, and mustard powder into the inner pot of the Instant Pot.

2. Secure the lid and set the vent to sealing. Manually set the cook time for 4 minutes.

3. When the cook time is over, manually release the pressure.

4. When the pin drops, remove the lid and stir in the cream, starting with ½ cup. Begin stirring in the shredded cheese, 1 cup at a time. If the sauce ends up being too thin, let it sit a while and it will thicken up.

Variation:

If you want the mac and cheese to have a crust on top, pour the mac and cheese from the Instant Pot into an oven-safe baking dish. Top with additional cheese and bake in a 325°F oven for about 15 minutes.

Macaroni and Velveeta Cheese

Lisa F. Good, Harrisonburg, VA

Makes 6 servings

Prep. Time: 10 minutes ❧ *Cooking Time: 2–3 hours* ❧ *Ideal slow-cooker size: 2- or 3-qt.*

1½ cups dry macaroni
1 Tbsp. butter
1 tsp. salt
½ lb. Velveeta Light cheese, sliced
4 cups milk

1. Combine macaroni, butter, and salt.

2. Layer cheese over top.

3. Pour in milk.

4. Cover. Cook on High for 2–3 hours, or until soft.

Pasta Primavera

Hope Comerford, Clinton Township, MI

Makes 6 servings
Prep. Time: 10 minutes & Cooking Time: 5 minutes (may vary due to pasta chosen)

2 cups chopped broccolini tops

½ lb. baby bella mushrooms, sliced

2 small zucchini, sliced into ¼-inch-thick rounds

1 cup sliced cherry tomatoes

3 garlic cloves, sliced

½ tsp. salt

⅛ tsp. pepper

2 Tbsp. olive oil, *divided*

8 oz. pasta of your choice

4 cups reduced-sodium vegetable stock

¼ cup grated reduced-fat Parmesan cheese

2 Tbsp. chopped fresh basil

1. In a large bowl, toss the broccolini, mushrooms, zucchini, cherry tomatoes, garlic, salt, and pepper with 1 tablespoon olive oil.

2. Set the Instant Pot to Sauté and heat the additional tablespoon of olive oil.

3. Pour the vegetables into the inner pot. Stir regularly for about 7 minutes, or until the vegetables are tender. Put them back in the large bowl you had them in and cover to keep them warm.

4. Press Cancel on the Instant Pot. Pour the pasta and vegetable stock into the inner pot and secure the lid. Set the vent to sealing.

5. Manually set the cook time for 5 minutes on high pressure, or half of whatever time the package instructions say to cook your pasta of choice for.

6. When the cooking time is over, manually release the pressure.

7. When the pin drops, remove the lid. Use a ladle to remove 1 cup of the cooking liquid. Pour this into the bowl with vegetables.

8. Wearing oven mitts, carefully remove the inner pot and drain the pasta into a colander.

9. Pour the drained pasta into the large bowl with the reserved cooking liquid and vegetables. Add the Parmesan cheese and fresh basil. Toss and enjoy!

Fresh Veggie Lasagna

Deanne Gingrich, Lancaster, PA

Makes 4–6 servings
Prep. Time: 30 minutes ❧ Cooking Time: 4 hours ❧ Ideal slow-cooker size: 4- or 5-qt.

1½ cups shredded low-fat mozzarella cheese

½ cup low-fat ricotta cheese

⅓ cup grated Parmesan cheese

1 egg, lightly beaten

1 tsp. dried oregano

¼ tsp. garlic powder

3 cups marinara sauce, *divided*

1 medium zucchini, diced, *divided*

4 uncooked lasagna noodles

4 cups fresh baby spinach, *divided*

1 cup fresh mushrooms, sliced, *divided*

1. Grease interior of slow-cooker crock.

2. In a bowl, mix the mozzarella, ricotta, and Parmesan cheeses, egg, oregano, and garlic powder. Set aside.

3. Spread ½ cup marinara sauce in crock.

4. Sprinkle with half the zucchini.

5. Spoon ⅓ of cheese mixture over zucchini.

6. Break 2 noodles into large pieces to cover cheese layer.

7. Spread ½ cup marinara over the noodles.

8. Top with half the spinach and then half the mushrooms.

9. Repeat layers, ending with cheese mixture, and then sauce. Press layers down firmly.

10. Cover and cook on Low for 4 hours, or until vegetables are as tender as you like them and noodles are fully cooked.

11. Let stand 15 minutes so lasagna can firm up before serving.

Meatless Ziti

Hope Comerford, Clinton Township, MI

Makes 8 servings
Prep. Time: 10 minutes & Cooking Time: 3 minutes

I Tbsp. olive oil

I small onion, chopped

3 cups water, *divided*

15-oz. can crushed tomatoes

8-oz. can tomato sauce

1½ tsp. Italian seasoning

I tsp. garlic powder

I tsp. onion powder

I tsp. sea salt

¼ tsp. pepper

12 oz. ziti

1–2 cups shredded mozzarella cheese

1. Set the Instant Pot to the Sauté function and heat the olive oil.

2. When the oil is hot, sauté the onion for 3 to 5 minutes, or until translucent.

3. Pour in 1 cup of the water and scrape any bits from the bottom of the inner pot with a wooden spoon or spatula.

4. In a bowl, mix the crushed tomatoes, tomato sauce, Italian seasoning, garlic powder, onion powder, sea salt, and pepper. Pour 1 cup of this in the inner pot and stir.

5. Pour in the ziti. Press it down so it's in there evenly, but *do not stir.*

6. Pour the remaining pasta sauce evenly over the top. Again, *do not stir.*

7. Secure the lid and set the vent to sealing. Manually set the cook time for 3 minutes.

8. When the cook time is over, let the pressure release naturally for 10 minutes, then manually release the remaining pressure.

9. When the pin drops, remove the lid and stir in the shredded mozzarella. This will thicken as it sits a bit.

Cheese Ravioli Casserole

Elizabeth Colucci, Lancaster, PA

Makes 4–6 servings
Prep Time: 30 minutes ⚜ Cooking Time: 2½–3 hours ⚜ Ideal slow-cooker size: 3-qt.

10-oz. pkg. cheese ravioli

16-oz. jar spaghetti sauce, with peppers, mushrooms, and onions, *divided*

½ cup Italian bread crumbs

1 cup mozzarella cheese

¼ cup **Parmesan cheese**, *optional*

½ cup cheddar cheese

1. Cook ravioli according to package directions. Drain.

2. Spoon enough spaghetti sauce into the slow cooker to cover the bottom. Place ravioli on top.

3. Cover with remaining sauce. Top with bread crumbs. Sprinkle with cheeses.

4. Stir to mix well.

5. Cover and cook on Low for 2½–3 hours, or until heated through, but without overcooking the pasta.

Tortellini with Broccoli

Susan Kasting, Jenks, OK

Makes 4 servings
Prep. Time: 10 minutes ❧ Cooking Time: 2½–3 hours ❧ Ideal slow-cooker size: 4-qt.

½ cup water

26-oz. jar your favorite pasta sauce, *divided*

1 Tbsp. Italian seasoning

9-oz. pkg. frozen spinach and cheese tortellini

16-oz. pkg. frozen broccoli florets

1. In a bowl, mix water, pasta sauce, and seasoning together.

2. Pour ⅓ of sauce into bottom of slow cooker. Top with all the tortellini.

3. Pour ⅓ of sauce over tortellini. Top with broccoli.

4. Pour remaining sauce over broccoli.

5. Cook on High for 2½–3 hours, or until broccoli and pasta are tender but not mushy.

Instant Pot Adaptation:

1. Place the frozen tortellini and broccoli florets into the inner pot of the Instant Pot.

2. Mix the pasta sauce with 1 cup of water and Italian seasoning (notice the increase in water). Pour this over the pasta and broccoli. *Do not stir.*

3. Secure the lid and set the vent to sealing. Set the cook time for 8 minutes on high pressure.

4. When cook time is over, manually release the pressure. When the pin drops, remove the lid. This will thicken as it sits with the lid off.

Pasta with Tomatoes, Olives, and Two Cheeses

Diane Clement, Rogers, AR

Makes 6–8 servings
Prep. Time: 30 minutes ⚜ *Cooking Time: 3 hours* ⚜ *Ideal slow-cooker size: 5- or 6-qt.*

1½ cups chopped onion

1 tsp. minced garlic

3 (28-oz.) cans Italian plum tomatoes, drained

2 tsp. dried basil

¼–½ tsp. red pepper flakes, according to the amount of heat you like

2 cups vegetable broth

Salt to taste

Pepper to taste

1 lb. uncooked penne or rigatoni

3 Tbsp. olive oil

2½ cups Havarti cheese

⅓ cup sliced, pitted, brine-cured olives (such as kalamata)

⅓ cup grated Parmesan cheese

¼ cup finely chopped fresh basil

1. Grease interior of slow-cooker crock.

2. Place onion, garlic, tomatoes, dried basil, and red pepper flakes in crock. Stir together well, breaking up tomatoes with back of spoon.

3. Stir in chicken broth.

4. Season with salt and pepper.

5. Cover. Cook on High for 2 hours.

6. Uncover. Continue cooking on High 1 hour, or until sauce is reduced to the consistency you like.

7. During last 30 minutes of cooking, prepare pasta according to package directions in a large stockpot until al dente.

8. Drain pasta and stir in olive oil. Cover and keep warm.

9. When sauce is done cooking, pour over pasta and toss to blend.

10. Stir in Havarti cheese and allow to melt.

11. Spoon into serving bowl. Top with olives and Parmesan cheese.

12. Sprinkle with fresh basil, then serve immediately.

Hot Tuna Macaroni Casserole

Dorothy VanDeest, Memphis, TN

Makes 6 servings
Prep. Time: 15 minutes ❧ *Cooking Time: 2–6 hours* ❧ *Ideal slow-cooker size: 3-qt.*

2 (6-oz.) cans water-packed tuna, rinsed and drained

1½ cups cooked macaroni

½ cup finely chopped onions

¼ cup finely chopped green bell peppers

4-oz. can sliced mushrooms, drained

10-oz. pkg. frozen cauliflower, partially thawed

½ cup low-sodium vegetable broth

1. Combine all ingredients in the slow cooker. Stir well.

2. Cover. Cook on Low for 4–6 hours or on High for 2–3 hours.

Main Dishes

Chicken Main Dishes

Garlic Galore Rotisserie Chicken

Hope Comerford, Clinton Township, MI

Makes 4 servings
Prep. Time: 5 minutes   Cooking Time: 33 minutes

3-lb. whole chicken

2 Tbsp. olive oil, *divided*

Salt to taste

Pepper to taste

20–30 fresh garlic cloves, peeled and left whole

1 cup chicken stock, broth, or water

2 Tbsp. garlic powder

2 tsp. onion powder

½ tsp. basil

½ tsp. cumin

½ tsp. chili powder

1. Rub chicken with 1 tablespoon of the olive oil and sprinkle with salt and pepper.

2. Place the garlic cloves inside the chicken. Use butcher's twine to secure the legs.

3. Press the Sauté button on the Instant Pot, then add the rest of the olive oil to the inner pot.

4. When the pot is hot, place the chicken inside. You are just trying to sear it, so leave it for about 4 minutes on each side.

5. Remove the chicken and set aside. Place the trivet at the bottom of the inner pot and pour in the chicken stock.

6. Mix together the remaining seasonings and rub it all over the entire chicken.

7. Place the chicken back inside the inner pot, breast side up, on top of the trivet and secure the lid to the sealing position.

8. Press the Manual button and use the +/- to set it for 25 minutes.

9. When the timer beeps, allow the pressure to release naturally for 15 minutes. If the lid will not open at this point, quick release the remaining pressure and remove the chicken.

10. Let the chicken rest for 5–10 minutes before serving.

Slow Cooked Honey Garlic Chicken Thighs

Colleen Heatwole, Burton, MI

Makes 2–4 servings
Prep. Time: 10 minutes ⚜ *Cooking Time: 4 hours* ⚜ *Ideal slow-cooker size: 3-quart*

4 boneless, skinless chicken thighs

2 Tbsp. soy sauce

½ cup ketchup

⅓ cup honey

3 garlic cloves, minced

1 tsp. basil

1. Place chicken thighs in bottom of crock.

2. Whisk remaining ingredients together in bowl and pour over chicken.

3. Cook covered on Low for 4 hours.

Basil Chicken

Phyllis Good, Lancaster, PA

Makes 4–6 servings
Prep. Time: 15 minutes ⚮ Cooking Time: 4¼–4½ hours ⚮ Ideal slow-cooker size: 4-qt.

2 pounds boneless, skinless chicken thighs

14½-oz. can diced tomatoes with juice

14½-oz. can garbanzo beans, rinsed and drained

2 Tbsp. capers with their brine

2 garlic cloves, sliced thinly

⅛ tsp. freshly ground pepper

1 tsp. dried basil

8 oz. crumbled feta cheese

¼ cup tightly packed basil leaves, chopped

1. Place chicken in the slow cooker. Pour tomatoes, garbanzos, and capers on top.

2. Sprinkle with garlic slices, pepper, and dried basil.

3. Cover and cook on Low for 4 hours.

4. Sprinkle with feta. Cook on Low for 15–30 more minutes, or until chicken is done.

5. Sprinkle with fresh basil and serve.

Serving suggestion:
Great served with pasta or crusty bread to handle the sauce.

SLOW COOKER

Balsamic Chicken

Hope Comerford, Clinton Township, MI

Makes 4 servings
Prep. Time: 10 minutes & Cooking Time: 5–6 hours & Ideal slow-cooker size: 3-qt.

2 lb. boneless, skinless chicken breasts

2 Tbsp. olive oil

½ tsp. salt

½ tsp. pepper

1 onion, halved and sliced

28-oz. can diced tomatoes

½ cup balsamic vinegar

2 tsp. sugar

2 tsp. garlic powder

2 tsp. Italian seasoning

1. Place chicken in crock. Drizzle with olive oil and sprinkle with salt and pepper.

2. Spread the onion over the top of the chicken.

3. In a bowl, mix together the diced tomatoes, balsamic vinegar, sugar, garlic powder, and Italian seasoning. Pour this over the chicken and onions.

4. Cover and cook on Low for 5–6 hours.

Serving suggestion:

Serve over cooked pasta or alongside your favorite vegetable and starch.

INSTANT POT

Butter Chicken

Jessica Stoner, Arlington, OH

Makes 4 servings
Prep. Time: 10–15 minutes ⚬ *Cooking Time: 20 minutes*

1 Tbsp. olive oil

1 medium onion, diced

1–2 medium garlic cloves, minced

½ Tbsp. minced ginger

1 tsp. garam masala

½ tsp. turmeric

2 tsp. kosher salt

2 lb. cubed boneless, skinless chicken breasts

¼ cup tomato paste

2 cups crushed tomatoes

1½ cups water

½ Tbsp. honey

1½ cups heavy cream

1 Tbsp. butter

1. On Sauté function at high heat, heat the oil in the inner pot of the Instant Pot. Add the onion, garlic, and ginger and sauté for 1 minute, until fragrant and onion is soft.

2. Add the garam masala, turmeric, and salt. Sauté quickly and add the chicken. Stir to coat chicken. Add the tomato paste and crushed tomatoes. Slowly add the water, scraping the bottom of the pot with a spoon to make sure there are no bits of tomato stuck to the bottom. Stir in the honey.

3. Secure the lid, making sure vent is turned to sealing function. Use the Poultry function and set cook time to 15 minutes. Once done cooking, do a quick release of the pressure.

4. Remove lid and change to medium/normal Sauté function and stir in the heavy cream and bring to a simmer. Simmer for 5 minutes, adding up to ¼ cup additional water if you need to thin the sauce out. Stir in the butter until melted and turn off.

Serving suggestion:

Serve hot with basmati rice and naan.

Barbecued Chicken

Charlotte Shaffer, East Earl, PA

Makes 6 servings
Prep. Time: 20 minutes ⚬ Cooking Time: 6–8 hours ⚬ Ideal slow-cooker size: 3- or 4-qt.

1 lb. frying chicken, cut up and skin removed (organic or free-range, if possible)

10¾-oz. can condensed tomato soup

¾ cup onion, chopped

¼ cup vinegar

3 Tbsp. brown sugar

1 Tbsp. Worcestershire sauce

½ tsp. salt

¼ tsp. dried basil

1. Place chicken in the slow cooker.

2. Combine all remaining ingredients and pour over chicken, making sure that the sauce glazes all the pieces.

3. Cover. Cook on Low for 6–8 hours.

Wild 'n Tangy Barbecue Chicken

Maria Shevlin, Sicklerville, NJ

Makes 4–6 servings
Prep. Time: 15 minutes & Cooking Time: 15 minutes

1–2 lb. boneless, skinless chicken thighs

1–2 lb. boneless, skinless chicken breasts

1 cup chicken broth

1 tsp. onion powder

1 tsp. garlic powder

½–1 tsp. chili powder

¼–½ tsp. red pepper flakes

½ tsp. smoked paprika

¼ cup brown sugar

½ cup onion, minced

1½ tsp. parsley flakes

2 garlic cloves, minced

18-oz. bottle of your favorite barbecue sauce

1. Place all the ingredients, except the barbecue sauce, into the inner pot of the Instant Pot.

2. Secure the lid and set the vent to sealing. Manually set the cook time for 15 minutes on high pressure.

3. When cook time is up, let the pressure release naturally for 10 minutes, then manually release the remaining pressure.

4. When the pin drops, remove the lid. Carefully drain most of the broth out and reserve it.

5. Shred the chicken in the pot with your hand mixer or between two forks. Note: The hand mixer works like a charm!

6. Add the barbecue sauce and mix well.

7. Taste and adjust seasonings if needed. If it's too dry for your liking, add some of the reserved liquid.

Serving suggestion:

Either serve on a plate, or on slider buns with a side of coleslaw and pickles. You can also try serving it open-faced on Texas toast.

Tuscan Chicken

Hope Comerford, Clinton Township, MI

Makes 4 servings
Prep. Time: 5 minutes   ✤   Cooking Time: 10 minutes

½ tsp. salt

½ tsp. onion powder

½ tsp. Italian seasoning

¼ tsp. pepper

2 lb. boneless, skinless chicken thighs

3 Tbsp. butter

6 garlic cloves, minced

¾ cup sliced baby bella mushrooms

¾ cup chicken stock

½ tsp. red pepper flakes

1 cup heavy cream

2 cups spinach

½ cup sliced sun-dried tomatoes

½ cup shredded Asiago cheese

1. Coat the chicken with the salt, onion powder, Italian seasoning, and pepper.

2. Set the Instant Pot to the Sauté function and let it get hot. Add the butter to melt.

3. When the butter is melted, immediately add the chicken to the inner pot to sear.

4. Once the chicken is seared on both sides, add the garlic and mushrooms. Sauté for about 1 minute.

5. Pour in the chicken stock and carefully deglaze the bottom of the pot, scraping up any stuck-on bits. Press Cancel.

6. Sprinkle in the red pepper flakes, then secure the lid and set the vent to sealing.

7. Manually set the cook time for 5 minutes on high pressure.

8. When cook time is up, manually release the pressure.

9. When the pin drops, remove the lid. Press Cancel, then Sauté. Remove the chicken and set aside.

10. Stir in the heavy cream slowly, then add the spinach, sun-dried tomatoes, and cheese. Once mixed, serve the chicken with the sauce over the top.

Serving suggestion:

Serve over your favorite pasta or rice.

Creamy Italian Chicken

Jo Zimmerman, Lebanon, PA

Makes 6 servings
Prep. Time: 10 minutes ⚜ Cooking Time: 4 hours ⚜ Ideal slow-cooker size: 3-qt.

2 lb. chicken tenders

1 envelope Italian salad dressing mix

¼ cup water

8-oz. pkg. cream cheese, cut into pieces

10½-oz. can condensed cream of chicken soup

4 oz. can sliced mushrooms, drained, *optional*

1. Place chicken in the slow cooker.

2. Combine dressing mix and water. Pour over chicken.

3. Cover and cook on Low for 3 hours.

4. Beat cream cheese and soup together and stir in mushrooms if you like. Pour over chicken and cook 1 hour longer.

Serving suggestion:
Serve over rice.

Instant Pot Adaptation:

1. Place the chicken in the inner pot of the Instant Pot. Pour 1 cup water (notice the increase), the cream of chicken soup, Italian dressing mix, and mushrooms, if desired, over the top. *Do not stir.*

2. Secure the lid and set the vent to sealing. Set the cook time for 25 minutes on high pressure.

3. When cook time is up, let the pressure release naturally for 7 minutes, then manually release the remaining pressure.

4. When the pin drops, remove the lid and stir in the cream cheese. Place the lid back on and let it sit for about 3 minutes.

5. Remove the lid and stir until the cream cheese is fully melted in.

Italian Chicken and Broccoli

Liz Clapper, Lancaster, PA

Makes 6 servings
Prep. Time: 15 minutes ⚬ Cooking Time: 5 minutes

1 Tbsp. olive oil

1 head broccoli, chopped into florets (about 4 cups)

2 garlic cloves, finely chopped

1 lb. chicken tenderloins

4 medium carrots, sliced thin

2 cups uncooked whole-grain macaroni pasta

3 cups low-fat, low-sodium chicken broth

1½ Tbsp. Italian seasoning

¼ cup shredded reduced-fat Parmesan cheese

1. Set the Instant Pot to Sauté and heat the oil.

2. Sauté the broccoli for 5 minutes in the inner pot. Set it aside in a bowl and cover to keep warm.

3. Add the garlic and chicken and sauté for 8 minutes.

4. Press Cancel. Add the carrots and stir. Pour the macaroni evenly over the top. Pour in the broth and Italian seasoning. *Do not stir.*

5. Secure the lid and set the vent to sealing.

6. Manually set the cook time for 5 minutes on high pressure.

7. When the cooking time is over, let the pressure release naturally for 5 minutes, then manually release the remaining pressure.

8. When the pin drops, remove the lid, sprinkle the contents with Parmesan, and serve immediately.

SLOW COOKER

Bacon-Feta Stuffed Chicken

Tina Goss, Duenweg, MO

Makes 4 servings
Prep. Time: 10 minutes   ♣   Cooking Time: 1½–3 hours   ♣   Ideal slow-cooker size: 3-qt.

¼ cup crumbled cooked bacon

¼ cup crumbled feta cheese

4 boneless, skinless chicken breast halves

2 (14½-oz.) cans diced tomatoes, undrained

1 Tbsp. dried basil

1. In a small bowl, mix bacon and cheese together lightly.

2. Cut a pocket in the thicker side of each chicken breast. Fill each with ¼ of the bacon and cheese mixture. Pinch shut and secure with toothpicks.

3. Place chicken in the slow cooker. Top with tomatoes and sprinkle with basil.

4. Cover and cook on High for 1½–3 hours, or until chicken is tender but not dry or mushy.

Chicken Marsala

Genelle Taylor, Perrysburg, OH

Makes 4 servings
Prep. Time: 10 minutes   ❧   Cooking Time: 5–6 hours   ❧   Ideal slow-cooker size: 5- or 6-qt.

4 boneless, skinless chicken breasts
Salt to taste
Pepper to taste
2 tsp. minced garlic
1 cup sliced mushrooms
1 cup sweet marsala cooking wine
½ cup water
¼ cup cornstarch
Fresh parsley, coarsely chopped

1. Lightly grease slow cooker with nonstick spray.

2. Season chicken with salt and pepper and place in the slow cooker.

3. Top chicken with garlic, mushrooms, and wine.

4. Cover and cook on Low for 5–6 hours.

5. Transfer chicken to a plate.

6. Whisk together water and cornstarch; then stir into slow cooker.

7. Add chicken back into slow cooker, switch heat to High, cover and cook another 20–30 minutes, until sauce is thickened.

8. Add salt and pepper as needed. Sprinkle with parsley and serve.

Chicken Parmigiana

Lois Ostrander, Lebanon, PA

Makes 6 servings
Prep. Time: 20 minutes   ♣   Cooking Time: 6–8 hours   ♣   Ideal slow-cooker size: 3½-qt.

1 egg
1 cup dry bread crumbs
6 bone-in chicken breast halves, *divided*
10½-oz. jar pizza sauce, *divided*
6 slices mozzarella cheese, or ½ cup grated Parmesan cheese

1. Beat egg in a shallow, oblong bowl. Place bread crumbs in another shallow, oblong bowl. Dip chicken halves into egg, and then into the crumbs, using a spoon to coat the meat on all sides with crumbs.

2. Sauté chicken in a large nonstick skillet sprayed with nonstick spray.

3. Arrange 1 layer of browned chicken in the slow cooker. Pour half the pizza sauce over top. Add a second layer of chicken. Pour remaining pizza sauce over top.

4. Cover and cook on Low for 5¾–7¾ hours, or until chicken is tender but not dry.

5. Add cheese on top. Cover and cook 15 more minutes.

Chicken and Dressing

Sharon Miller, Holmesville, OH

Makes 10–12 servings
Prep. Time: 30 minutes ⚬ *Cooking Time: 4¾–8¾ hours* ⚬ *Ideal slow-cooker size: 6-qt.*

12–13 cups slightly dry bread cubes

1–2 cups chopped onion

2 cups diced celery

4 Tbsp. butter, melted

1 tsp. poultry seasoning

½ tsp. dried thyme

1½ tsp. salt

½ tsp. pepper

3 cups shredded or diced cooked chicken

3 well-beaten eggs

3½–4½ cups low-sodium chicken broth

1. Place bread cubes in a large bowl.

2. Sauté onion and celery in melted butter. Stir in poultry seasoning, thyme, salt, and pepper.

3. Toss in the cooked chicken.

4. Pour entire chicken mixture over bread cubes and toss well together.

5. Add the eggs.

6. Stir in chicken broth to moisten. Pack lightly into slow cooker.

7. Cover and cook on High for 45 minutes. Reduce heat to Low and cook for 4–8 hours.

Serving suggestion:

A green vegetable and cranberry sauce would make a nice accompaniment to this dish.

Chicken and Dumplings

Annabelle Unternahrer, Shipshewana, IN

Makes 5–6 servings
Prep. Time: 25 minutes & Cooking Time: 2½–3½ hours & Ideal slow-cooker size: 3- or 4-qt.

1 lb. uncooked boneless, skinless chicken breasts, cut in 1-inch cubes

1 lb. frozen vegetables of your choice

1 medium onion, diced

3 cups chicken broth, *divided*

1½ cups low-fat buttermilk biscuit mix

1. Combine chicken, vegetables, onion, and chicken broth (reserve ½ cup + 1 tablespoon broth) in the slow cooker.

2. Cover. Cook on High for 2–3 hours.

3. Mix biscuit mix with reserved broth until moistened. Drop by tablespoonfuls over hot chicken and vegetables.

4. Cover. Cook on High for 10 minutes.

5. Uncover. Cook on High for 20 minutes more.

Creamy Chicken Rice Casserole

Wanda Roth, Napoleon, OH

Makes 8 servings
Prep. Time: 20 minutes ⚶ *Cooking Time: 2–6 hours* ⚶ *Ideal slow-cooker size: 6-qt.*

1 cup long-grain rice, uncooked

3 cups water

2 tsp. low-sodium chicken bouillon granules

10¾-oz. can cream of chicken soup

2 cups chopped, cooked chicken breast

¼ tsp. garlic powder

1 tsp. onion salt

1 cup grated cheddar cheese

16-oz. bag frozen broccoli, thawed

1. Combine all ingredients except broccoli in the slow cooker.

2. Cook on High for 2–3 hours or on Low for 4–6 hours.

3. One hour before end of cooking time, stir in broccoli.

INSTANT POT

Chicken Stir-Fry

Hope Comerford, Clinton Township, MI

Makes 4–6 servings
Prep. Time: 5 minutes ♣ *Cooking Time: 16 minutes*

2 lb. boneless, skinless chicken breasts

1 small onion, sliced

½ cup soy sauce or Liquid Aminos

¼ cup chicken stock

1 clove garlic, minced

1 tsp. ginger

⅛ tsp. pepper

¼ cup cornstarch

¼ cup cold water

20-oz. bag frozen stir-fry vegetables

Cooked rice

1. Place the chicken into the inner pot of the Instant Pot, along with the onion, soy sauce, chicken stock, garlic, ginger, and pepper.

2. Secure the lid and set the vent to sealing. Manually set the cook time for 7 minutes on high pressure. (This would be a good time to start the rice on the stove, or in a second Instant Pot.)

3. When cook time is up, let the pressure release naturally for 2 minutes, then release the rest of the pressure manually.

4. When the pin drops, remove the lid. Remove the chicken and shred it.

5. Switch the Instant Pot to the Sauté function. Mix the cornstarch and water in a small bowl, then stir it into the liquid in the pot. Add the frozen vegetables and continue to let things simmer and stir for another 7 minutes or so.

6. Stir the chicken back into the pot and serve over cooked rice.

Pineapple Chicken

Amanda Gross, Souderton, PA

Makes 3–4 servings
Prep. Time: 5 minutes ⚘ *Cooking Time: 10 minutes*

4 boneless, skinless chicken thighs, cut into 1½-inch pieces

¼ cup soy sauce

½ cup pineapple juice

½ cup ketchup

2 Tbsp. white vinegar

16-oz. can crushed pineapple

1 cup chicken stock or water

1. Place all ingredients into the inner pot of the Instant Pot in the order listed.

2. Secure the lid and set the vent to sealing. Manually set the cook time for 10 minutes on high pressure.

3. When cook time is up, let the pressure release naturally for 10 minutes, then manually release the remaining pressure.

Serving Suggestion:
Serve over cooked rice.

Slow-Cooker Adaptation:

1. Place all ingredients into a 4-quart slow cooker with only ½ cup chicken stock or water (notice the reduction).

2. Place the lid on the crock and cook on Low for 4–5 hours.

Salsa Ranch Chicken with Black Beans

Hope Comerford, Clinton Township, MI

Makes 8 servings
Prep. Time: 10 minutes ⚬ Cooking Time: 5–6 hours ⚬ Ideal slow-cooker size: 3-qt.

2 large boneless, skinless chicken breasts

1-oz. packet low-sodium taco seasoning

1 oz. packet dry ranch dressing mix

1 cup salsa

10½-oz. can condensed cream of chicken soup

15-oz. can black beans, drained, rinsed

Sour cream, *optional*

Shredded cheese, *optional*

1. Place chicken in crock.

2. In a bowl, mix together the taco seasoning, ranch dressing mix, salsa, cream of chicken soup, and black beans. Pour over the chicken.

3. Cover and cook on Low for 5–6 hours.

4. Serve with sour cream and cheese, if desired.

Serving suggestion:
Serve on top of rice or in a tortilla.

Sweet-and-Sour Chicken

Janette Fox, Honey Brook, PA

Makes 6–8 servings
Prep. Time: 15 minutes ❧ Cooking Time: 4 hours ❧ Ideal slow-cooker size: 5-qt.

3 lb. boneless, skinless chicken thighs

½ cup chopped onions

½ green pepper, chopped

15-oz. can pineapple chunks in juice

¾ cup ketchup

¼ cup brown sugar, packed

2 Tbsp. apple cider vinegar

2 tsp. soy sauce

½ tsp. garlic salt

½ tsp. salt

¼ tsp. pepper

Cooked rice

1. Grease interior of slow-cooker crock.

2. Put chicken in crock. If you need to add a second layer, stagger the pieces so they don't directly overlap each other.

3. Scatter onions and green pepper over top.

4. In a mixing bowl, combine pineapple chunks and juice, ketchup, brown sugar, vinegar, soy sauce, garlic salt, salt, and pepper.

5. Spoon over chicken, onions, and green pepper.

6. Cover. Cook on Low for 4 hours, or until instant-read meat thermometer registers 165°F when stuck into center of thighs.

7. Serve over cooked rice.

Salsa Lime Chicken

Maria Shevlin, Sicklerville, NJ

Makes 2–4 servings
Prep. Time: 10 minutes ❧ Cooking Time: 17 minutes

4 bone-in, skin-on chicken thighs

I tsp. chili lime seasoning

½ tsp. True Lime Garlic Cilantro Spice Blend

2 tsp. olive oil

I cup diced onion

I cup chicken broth

1½ cups of your favorite salsa

I lime, zested and juiced

2 tsp. garlic powder

2 pkg. True Lime Crystallized Lime Packets

¼ cup brown sugar

1. Season both sides of chicken with chili lime seasoning and cilantro lime seasoning.

2. Set the Instant Pot to Sauté and let it get hot.

3. Add the olive oil to the inner pot, then sauté the chicken, skin-side down, for 3–4 minutes.

4. Turn the chicken over to brown on other side.

5. Add the onion, broth, salsa, lime juice and zest, garlic powder, lime crystals, and brown sugar. Scrape the bottom of the pot and give it a quick stir.

6. Secure the lid and set the vent to sealing. Manually set the cook time for 9 minutes on high pressure.

7. When cook time is up, manually release the pressure.

Serving suggestions:
Serve with green beans and warm tortillas.

Slow-Cooker Adaptation:

1. Season both sides of chicken with chili lime seasoning and cilantro lime seasoning, then place them into a 5-quart slow cooker.

2. Omit the olive oil. Place all remaining ingredients into the slow cooker on top of the chicken.

3. Place the lid on the crock and cook on Low for 5 hours.

SLOW COOKER

Shredded Lime Chicken

Mary Seielstad, Sparks, NV
Hope Comerford, Clinton Township, MI

Makes 6 servings
Prep. Time: 10 minutes ⚬ Cooking Time: 5–6 hours ⚬ Ideal slow-cooker size: 3-qt.

1½ lb. boneless, skinless chicken breasts

2 limes, juiced

1 Tbsp. chili powder

1 tsp. salt

2 tsp. fresh minced garlic

16-oz. jar salsa of your choosing

1 small onion, chopped

1 cup frozen corn

1. Place chicken breasts in crock.

2. In a bowl, mix the remaining ingredients. Pour this over the chicken.

3. Cover and cook on Low for 5–6 hours.

4. Remove chicken and shred between two forks. Stir back through juices in the crock.

Serving suggestion:

This is great in tacos or on top of nachos.

Chicken Enchiladas

Jennifer Yoder Sommers, Harrisonburg, VA

Makes 4 servings
Prep. Time: 20 minutes ❧ Cooking Time: 4 hours ❧ Ideal slow-cooker size: 3-qt.

2 (10¾-oz.) cans cream of chicken or mushroom soup

4½-oz. can diced green chilies

2–3 boneless, skinless whole chicken breasts, cut into pieces

2 cups shredded cheddar cheese

5 (6-inch) flour tortillas

1. In a mixing bowl, combine soup, chilies, and chicken.

2. Spray the interior of the cooker with nonstick cooking spray.

3. Spoon in 1/5 of the chicken mixture on the bottom. Top with 1/5 of the cheese and then 1 tortilla. Continue layering in that order, and with those amounts, four more times, ending with cheese on top.

4. Cover cooker and cook on Low for 4 hours.

Easy Enchilada Shredded Chicken

Hope Comerford, Clinton Township, MI

Makes 10–14 servings
Prep. Time: 10 minutes ⚘ Cooking Time: 10 minutes

5 lb. boneless, skinless chicken thighs, cut into 1½-inch pieces

14½-oz. can petite diced tomatoes

1 medium onion, chopped

8 oz. red enchilada sauce

½ tsp. salt

½ tsp. chili powder

½ tsp. basil

½ tsp. garlic powder

¼ tsp. pepper

1 cup chicken stock

Plain yogurt for garnish, *optional*

Fresh cilantro for garnish, *optional*

1. Place all the ingredients, except the garnishes, into the inner pot of the Instant Pot.

2. Secure the lid and set the vent to sealing. Manually set the cook time for 10 minutes on high pressure.

3. When cook time is up, let the pressure release naturally for 10 minutes, then manually release the remaining pressure.

4. Remove the lid. Take the chicken pieces out, shred the chicken between two forks, and mix the chicken back into the juices in the pot.

5. Serve with the yogurt and cilantro if desired.

Serving suggestions:

Serve over salad, brown rice, quinoa, sweet potatoes, nachos, or soft-shell corn tortillas.

Slow-Cooker Adaptation:

1. Place all the ingredients, except the garnishes, into a 7–8 quart slow cooker.

2. Place the lid on the crock and cook on Low for 5 hours.

3. Continue with steps 4 and 5 above.

Slow-Cooker Burritos

SLOW COOKER

Hope Comerford, Clinton Township, MI

Makes 8 servings
Prep. Time: 10 minutes ⚜ *Cooking Time: 5 hours* ⚜ *Ideal slow-cooker size: 3-qt.*

1½ lb. boneless, skinless chicken breasts

15-oz. can pinto beans, rinsed and drained

2 cups salsa

1 cup chicken stock

1 small onion, chopped

4-oz. can diced green chilies

1 cup frozen corn

2 Tbsp. chili powder

1 tsp. cumin

1½ tsp. salt

½ cup brown rice

8 round flour tortillas

1. Place the chicken in the crock.

2. In a bowl, mix the pinto beans, salsa, chicken stock, onion, green chilies, corn, chili powder, cumin, and salt. Pour this over the chicken.

3. Cover and cook on Low for 3 hours. Stir in the rice.

4. Cover again and cook on Low for an additional 2 hours.

5. Remove and shred the chicken between two forks. Stir it back through the contents of the crock.

6. Fill each tortilla with the burrito filling and wrap them up.

Jazzed-Up Pulled Chicken

Hope Comerford, Clinton Township, MI

Makes 6–8 servings
Prep. Time: 5 minutes ⚶ Cooking Time: 6–7 hours ⚶ Ideal slow-cooker size: 4-qt.

2 lb. boneless, skinless chicken breasts

1 cup ketchup

¼ cup molasses

2 Tbsp. apple cider vinegar

2 Tbsp. Worcestershire sauce

1 clove garlic, minced

2 tsp. dry mustard

2 Tbsp. orange juice

1 tsp. orange zest

Serving suggestion:
Serve on buns with your favorite toppings.

1. Place chicken in crock.

2. In a bowl, mix the ketchup, molasses, apple cider vinegar, Worcestershire sauce, minced garlic, mustard powder, orange juice, and orange zest. Pour over the chicken.

3. Cover and cook on Low for 6–7 hours.

4. Remove the chicken and shred between two forks, then stir back through the sauce in the crock.

Instant Pot Adaptation:

1. In the inner pot of the Instant Pot, mix the ketchup, molasses, apple cider vinegar, Worcestershire sauce, minced garlic, mustard powder, orange juice, and orange zest. Add an additional cup of liquid of your choice (orange juice, water, chicken stock).

2. Place the chicken into the mixture in the pot.

3. Secure the lid and set the vent to sealing. Set the cook time for 16 minutes on high pressure.

4. When the cook time is over, let the pressure release naturally for 10 minutes, then manually release the remaining pressure.

5. Remove the chicken and shred between two forks, then stir back through the sauce in the pot. Garnish with cilantro, shredded carrots, and peanuts, if desired.

Mild Chicken Curry with Coconut Milk

Brittney Horst, Lititz, PA

Makes 4–6 servings
Prep. Time: 10 minutes ⚬ *Cooking Time: 14 minutes*

1 large onion, diced

6 garlic cloves, crushed

¼ cup coconut oil

½ tsp. pepper

½ tsp. turmeric

½ tsp. paprika

¼ tsp. cinnamon

¼ tsp. cloves

¼ tsp. cumin

¼ tsp. ginger

½ tsp. salt

1 Tbsp. curry powder (more if you like more flavor)

½ tsp. chili powder

24-oz. can low-sodium diced or crushed tomatoes

13½-oz. can light coconut milk

4 lb. boneless, skinless chicken breasts, cut into chunks

1. Sauté onion and garlic in the coconut oil, either with Sauté setting in the inner pot of the Instant Pot or on stove top, then add to pot.

2. Combine spices in a small bowl, then add to the inner pot.

3. Add tomatoes and coconut milk and stir.

4. Add chicken and stir to coat the pieces with the sauce.

5. Secure the lid and make sure vent is at sealing. Set to Manual mode (or Pressure Cook on newer models) for 14 minutes.

6. Let pressure release naturally (if you're crunched for time, you can do a quick release).

7. Serve with your favorite sides and enjoy!

Serving suggestion:
We like it on rice, with a couple of veggies on the side.

Slow-Cooker Adaptation:

1. Place all ingredients except the chicken into a 5-quart slow cooker and stir. Add the chicken into the sauce, coating it.

2. Cover the crock and cook on Low for 6 hours.

INSTANT POT

Thai Chicken Rice Bowls

Vonnie Oyer, Hubbard, OR

Makes 4–6 servings
Prep. Time: 15 minutes ⚬ *Cooking Time: 20 minutes*

2 Tbsp. olive oil

2 lb. chicken breasts (about 4)

½ cup sweet chili Thai sauce

3 Tbsp. soy sauce

½ Tbsp. fish sauce

½ Tbsp. minced ginger

½ Tbsp. minced garlic

1 tsp. lime juice

1 tsp. sriracha sauce

1 Tbsp. peanut butter

1 cup uncooked long-grain white rice

2 cups broth

Garnishes:

Cilantro, *optional*

Shredded carrots, *optional*

Peanuts, *optional*

1. Select the Sauté setting on the Instant Pot and add the olive oil to the inner pot.

2. Sear the chicken for 2–3 minutes on both sides to seal in their juices. Remove to a glass baking dish and press Cancel.

3. Mix the sweet chili Thai sauce, soy sauce, fish sauce, ginger, garlic, lime juice, sriracha, and peanut butter together.

4. Pour the sauce over the chicken breasts in glass dish.

5. Place the rice in the inner pot of the Instant Pot and add the chicken and sauce over top.

6. Add the broth and secure the lid. Make sure vent is on sealing.

7. Select the Manual setting (on high pressure) and set the timer to 10 minutes. Let pressure release naturally.

8. Take out and shred the chicken with two forks. Mix the chicken back in with the rice.

Turkey Main Dishes

Maple-Glazed Turkey Breast with Rice

Jeanette Oberholtzer, Manheim, PA

Makes 4 servings
Prep Time: 10–15 minutes ⚭ *Cooking Time: 4–6 hours* ⚭ *Ideal slow-cooker size: 3- to 4-qt.*

6-oz. pkg. long-grain wild rice mix

1½ cups water

2-lb. boneless turkey breast, cut into
1½–2-inch chunks

¼ cup maple syrup

1 onion, chopped

¼ tsp. ground cinnamon

½ tsp. salt, *optional*

1. Combine all ingredients in the slow cooker.

2. Cook on Low for 4–6 hours, or until turkey and rice are both tender, but not dry or mushy.

Turkey Meatloaf

Delores A. Gnagey, Saginaw, MI

Makes 4–5 servings
Prep. Time: 15 minutes ⚘ *Cooking Time: 15 minutes*

1 cup + 1 Tbsp. water, *divided*

1 lb. lean ground turkey

½ small onion, minced

1½ Tbsp. minced fresh parsley

2 egg whites

2 Tbsp. skim milk

½ tsp. dry mustard

¼ tsp. salt

⅛ tsp. ground white pepper

Pinch nutmeg

1 slice whole wheat bread, lightly toasted, made into coarse crumbs

1 Tbsp. low-sugar ketchup

1. Set the trivet inside the inner pot of the Instant Pot and pour in 1 cup water.

2. In a medium bowl, mix the ground turkey, onion, and parsley. Set aside.

3. In another bowl, whisk the egg whites. Add the milk, mustard, salt, white pepper, and nutmeg to the egg. Whisk to blend.

4. Add the bread crumbs to the egg mixture. Let rest 10 minutes.

5. Add the egg mixture to the meat mixture and blend well.

6. Spray the inside of a 7-inch springform baking pan, then spread the meat mixture into it.

7. Blend together the ketchup and 1 tablespoon water in a small bowl. Spread the mixture on top of the meat. Cover the pan with aluminum foil.

8. Place the springform pan on top of the trivet inside the inner pot.

9. Secure the lid and set the vent to sealing.

10. Manually set the cook time for 15 minutes on high pressure.

11. When the cooking time is over, let the pressure release naturally.

12. When the pin drops, remove the lid and use oven mitts to carefully remove the trivet from the inner pot.

13. Allow the meat to stand 10 minutes before slicing to serve.

Cheesy Stuffed Cabbage

Maria Shevlin, Sicklerville, NJ

Makes 6–8 servings
Prep. Time: 30 minutes ❧ Cooking Time: 18 minutes

1–2 heads Savoy cabbage
1 lb. ground turkey
1 egg
1 cup shredded cheddar cheese
2 Tbsp. heavy cream
¼ cup shredded Parmesan cheese
¼ cup shredded mozzarella cheese
¼ cup finely diced onion
¼ cup finely diced bell pepper
¼ cup finely diced mushrooms
1 tsp. salt
½ tsp. pepper
1 tsp. garlic powder
6 basil leaves, fresh and cut chiffonade
1 Tbsp. fresh parsley, chopped
1 qt. of your favorite pasta sauce

1. Remove the core from the cabbages.

2. Boil water and place 1 head at a time into the water for approximately 10 minutes.

3. Allow cabbage to cool slightly. Once cooled, remove the leaves carefully and set aside. You'll need about 15 or 16.

4. Mix together the meat and all remaining ingredients except the pasta sauce.

5. One leaf at a time, put a heaping tablespoon of meat mixture in the center.

6. Tuck the sides in and then roll tightly.

7. Add ½ cup sauce to the bottom of the inner pot of the Instant Pot.

8. Place the rolls, fold-side down, into the pot and layer them, putting a touch of sauce between each layer and finally on top. (You may want to cook the rolls a half batch at a time.)

9. Lock lid and make sure vent is at sealing. Set timer on 18 minutes on Manual at high pressure, then manually release the pressure when cook time is over.

Slow-Cooker Adaptation:

1. Follow steps 1–6 above.

2. Add ½ cup sauce to the bottom of a 7-quart slow cooker, then place the rolls, fold-side down, into the crock, tightly together. Layer them, putting a touch of sauce between each layer and finally on top.

3. Cover the crock and cook on Low for 8 hours.

Pizza in a Pot

Marianne J. Troyer, Millersburg, OH

Makes 8 servings
Prep. Time: 25 minutes ⚓ Cooking Time: 15 minutes

1 pound bulk lean sweet Italian turkey sausage, browned and drained

28-oz. can crushed tomatoes

15½-oz. can chili beans

2¼-oz. can sliced black olives, drained

1 medium onion, chopped

1 small green bell pepper, chopped

2 garlic cloves, minced

¼ cup grated Parmesan cheese

1 Tbsp. quick-cooking tapioca

1 Tbsp. dried basil

1 bay leaf

1. Set the Instant Pot to Sauté, then add the turkey sausage. Sauté until browned.

2. Add the remaining ingredients into the Instant Pot and stir.

3. Secure the lid and make sure the vent is set to sealing. Cook on Manual for 15 minutes.

4. When cook time is up, let the pressure release naturally for 5 minutes, then perform a quick release. Discard bay leaf.

Serving Suggestion:

Serve over pasta. Top with mozzarella cheese.

Slow-Cooker Adaptation:

1. Combine all ingredients in a 4- or 5-qt. slow cooker.

2. Cover. Cook on Low for 8–9 hours.

3. Discard bay leaf. Stir well.

Kielbasa and Cabbage

Mary Ann Lefever, Lancaster, PA

Makes 4 servings
Prep. Time: 10–15 minutes ⚜ *Cooking Time: 8 hours* ⚜ *Ideal slow-cooker size: 4- or 5-qt.*

1 lb. turkey kielbasa, cut into 4 chunks

4 large white potatoes, cut into chunks

1-lb. head green cabbage, shredded

1 qt. whole tomatoes (strained if you don't like seeds)

1 medium onion, thinly sliced, *optional*

1. Layer kielbasa, then potatoes, and then cabbage into slow cooker.

2. Pour tomatoes over top.

3. Top with sliced onion if you wish.

4. Cover. Cook on High for 8 hours, or until meat is cooked through and vegetables are as tender as you like them.

Tip:

If desired, brown kielbasa in a skillet over medium heat before adding to slow cooker.

Instant Pot Adaptation:

1. If desired, you may use the Sauté function to brown the kielbasa with cooking oil of your choice before adding everything else. If you decide to do this, add about ¼ cup of liquid at the end and scrape any brown bits off the bottom of the inner pot. If you do not want to take the time to do this, skip to the next step.

2. Add all the ingredients into the inner pot of the Instant Pot and stir. Add 1 cup water. (Notice this is an addition to the ingredient list.)

3. Secure the lid and set the vent to sealing. Set the cook time for 15 minutes on high pressure.

4. When cook time is up, manually release the pressure. When the pin drops, remove the lid and serve.

Pork Main Dishes

Carolina Pot Roast

Jonathan Gehman, Harrisonburg, VA

Makes 3–4 servings
Prep. Time: 20 minutes ⚜ *Cooking Time: 3 hours* ⚜ *Ideal slow-cooker size: 3-qt.*

3 medium-large sweet potatoes, peeled and cut into 1-inch chunks

¼ cup brown sugar

1-lb. pork roast

Scant ¼ tsp. cumin

Sea salt to taste

Water

1. Place sweet potatoes in bottom of slow cooker. Sprinkle brown sugar over potatoes.

2. Heat nonstick skillet over medium-high heat. Add roast and brown on all sides. Sprinkle meat with cumin and salt while browning. Place pork on top of potatoes.

3. Add an inch of water to the cooker, being careful not to wash the seasoning off the meat.

4. Cover and cook on Low for 3 hours, or until meat and potatoes are tender but not dry or mushy.

Instant Pot Adaptation:

1. Using the Sauté function on the Instant Pot, heat 1 tablespoon oil of your choice.
2. Sprinkle the pork roast with the cumin and salt. Sear the pork on all sides, then remove it and set aside.
3. Add ½ cup water to the bottom of the inner pot and scrape off any cooked-on bits. Press Cancel.
4. Place the sweet potatoes into the inner pot and sprinkle with brown sugar. Place the pork roast on top.
5. Pour in an additional ½ cup water.
6. Secure the lid and set the vent to sealing. Set the cook time for 15 minutes on high pressure.
7. When cook time is up, let the pressure release naturally for 15 minutes, then manually release any remaining pressure. When the pin drops, remove the lid.

Cranberry Jalapeño Pork Roast

Hope Comerford, Clinton Township, MI

Makes 4–6 servings
Prep. Time: 10 minutes   ❧   Cooking Time: 7–8 hours   ❧   Ideal slow-cooker size: 3-qt.

2–3-lb. pork roast
1 tsp. garlic powder
½ tsp. salt
½ tsp. pepper
1 small onion, chopped
½ jalapeño, seeded and diced
14-oz. can jellied cranberry sauce

1. Place pork roast in crock.

2. Season the pork roast with the garlic powder, salt, and pepper.

3. Dump in the onion and jalapeño.

4. Spoon the jellied cranberry sauce over the top of the contents of the crock.

5. Cover and cook on Low for 7–8 hours.

Easy Pork Loin

Colleen Heatwole, Burton, MI

Makes 4–5 servings
Prep. Time: 5 minutes ⚱ Cooking Time: 20 minutes

1½-lb. pork loin
2 Tbsp. soy sauce
2 Tbsp. tamari
¼ tsp. ground ginger
½ tsp. garlic powder
1 cup chicken stock or white wine

1. Add all ingredients into the inner pot of the Instant Pot in the order listed.

2. Secure the lid and set the vent to sealing. Manually set the cook time for 20 minutes on high pressure.

3. When cook time is up, let the pressure release naturally for 10 minutes, then manually release any remaining pressure.

4. If desired, meat may be shredded before serving.

Serving suggestion:
This goes well with sweet potatoes.

Slow-Cooker Adaptation:

1. Place all ingredients into a 3-quart slow cooker. You can reduce the chicken stock to ½ cup.
2. Cover and cook on Low for 5–6 hours.
3. If desired, meat may be shredded before serving.

Cranberry Pork Tenderloin

Janice Yoskovich, Carmichaels, PA

Makes 8 servings
Prep. Time: 10 minutes   ♣   Cooking Time: 4 hours   ♣   Ideal slow-cooker size: 4-qt.

1½-lb. pork tenderloin
12 oz. chili sauce
16-oz. can jellied cranberry sauce
2 Tbsp. brown sugar
5 cups cooked long-grain enriched rice

1. Place pork tenderloin in the slow cooker.

2. Mix together chili sauce, cranberry sauce, and brown sugar. Pour over pork.

3. Cover and cook on Low for 4 hours, or until cooked through but not dry.

4. Serve over rice.

Tropical Pork with Yams

SLOW COOKER · **INSTANT POT ADAPTATION**

Hope Comerford, Clinton Township, MI

Makes 6 servings
Prep. Time: 15 minutes ☙ Cooking Time: 7–8 hours ☙ Ideal slow-cooker size: 5-qt.

2–3-lb. pork loin

Salt to taste

Pepper to taste

20-oz. can crushed pineapple

¼ cup honey

¼ cup brown sugar

¼ cup apple cider vinegar

1 tsp. low-sodium soy sauce

4 yams, peeled and cut into bite-sized chunks

1. Spray crock with nonstick spray.

2. Lay pork loin at the bottom of the crock, and season it with salt and pepper on both sides.

3. In a separate bowl, combine pineapple, honey, brown sugar, apple cider vinegar, and soy sauce. Mix.

4. Place chunks of yams over and around the pork loin, and then pour pineapple sauce over the top.

5. Cover and cook on Low for 7–8 hours.

Instant Pot Adaptation:

1. Lay pork loin at the bottom of the inner pot of the Instant Pot, and season it with salt and pepper on both sides.

2. In a separate bowl, combine pineapple, honey, brown sugar, apple cider vinegar, and soy sauce. Add an additional ¾ cup of liquid (pineapple juice, apple juice, water, or broth are good choices).

3. Place chunks of yams over and around the pork loin, and then pour pineapple sauce over the top.

4. Secure the lid and set the vent to sealing. Set the cook time for 5 minutes on high pressure.

5. When cook time is up, let the pressure release naturally for 10 minutes, then manually release any remaining pressure. When the pin drops, remove the lid.

Tomato-Glazed Pork with Grilled Corn Salsa

Janet Melvin, Cincinnati, OH

Makes 6–8 servings

Prep. Time: 45 minutes & Cooking Time: 3–4 hours & Ideal slow-cooker size: 5-qt.

Tomato glaze:

2 Tbsp. dry mustard

1 Tbsp. ground ginger

1 Tbsp. ground fennel

1 Tbsp. minced garlic

¼ cup mayonnaise

1 cup ketchup

¼ cup honey

1 Tbsp. Worcestershire sauce

¼ cup grated fresh horseradish

3 Tbsp. white wine mustard

2 Tbsp. minced capers

1 Tbsp. Tabasco sauce

2-lb. boneless pork loin roast, short and wide in shape

Salsa:

3 ears sweet corn, husked and silked, or 4 cups frozen or canned corn

½ cup olive oil

¼ cup chopped sun-dried tomatoes

1 clove garlic, minced

½ cup wild mushrooms, sliced

2 Tbsp. chopped fresh cilantro

2 Tbsp. fresh lime juice

1 chipotle pepper in adobo sauce, finely chopped

½ tsp. salt

1. Grease interior of slow-cooker crock.

2. Prepare glaze by mixing the dry mustard, ginger, fennel, garlic, and mayonnaise.

3. When well blended, stir in remaining glaze ingredients.

4. Place pork in the slow cooker, fat-side up. Cover with glaze.

5. Cover. Cook on Low for 3–4 hours, or until instant-read meat thermometer registers 140°F when stuck into center of roast.

6. While roast is cooking, brush ears of corn with olive oil. Wrap in foil.

7. Bake at 350°F for 15 minutes. Unwrap and grill or broil until evenly browned.

8. Cool. Cut kernels from cob.

9. Combine corn with rest of salsa ingredients.

10. Cover and refrigerate until ready to use.

11. When pork is finished cooking, remove from cooker to cutting board. Cover with foil and let stand for 10 minutes.

12. Slice and serve on top of grilled corn salsa.

Easiest Ever Barbecue Country Ribs

Hope Comerford, Clinton Township, MI

Makes 4–6 servings
Prep. Time: 5 minutes ♣ Cooking Time: 8–10 hours ♣ Ideal slow-cooker size: 6-qt.

4 lb. boneless country-style ribs

Salt to taste

Pepper to taste

18-oz. bottle of your favorite barbecue sauce

1. Place the country ribs into the crock and sprinkle them with salt and pepper on both sides.

2. Pour half the bottle of barbecue sauce on one side of the ribs. Flip them over and pour the other half of the sauce on the other side of the ribs. Spread it around.

3. Cover and cook on Low for 8–10 hours.

Pork Baby Back Ribs

Marla Folkerts, Batavia, IL

Makes 6–8 servings
Prep. Time: 20 minutes ☙ Cooking Time: 30 minutes

3 racks of ribs
I cup brown sugar
I cup white sugar
I tsp. garlic powder
I tsp. garlic salt
I cup water
½ cup apple cider vinegar
I tsp. liquid smoke
½ cup barbecue sauce

1. Take the membrane/skin off the back of the ribs.

2. Mix together the remaining ingredients (except the barbecue sauce) and slather it on the ribs.

3. Place the ribs around the inside of the inner pot instead of stacking them. Secure the lid in place and make sure vent is at sealing.

4. Use the Meat setting and set for 30 minutes on high pressure.

5. When cooking time is up, let the pressure release naturally for 10 minutes, then do a quick release of the remaining pressure.

6. Place the ribs on a baking sheet and cover them with the barbecue sauce. Broil for 7–10 minutes (watching so they don't burn).

Tip:

I think placing the ribs around the pot instead of stacking makes it easier.

Pork Chops in Gravy

Hope Comerford, Clinton Township, MI

Makes 6 servings
Prep. Time: 10 minutes ✿ Cooking Time: 20 minutes

1 Tbsp. olive oil

½ cup sliced onion

6 boneless pork chops,
1–1½ inches thick

Salt to taste

Pepper to taste

1½ cups beef broth, *divided*

1 tsp. Worcestershire sauce

½ tsp. low-sodium soy sauce

1 tsp. garlic powder

1 tsp. onion powder

2 tsp. cornstarch

2 tsp. cold water

½ cup sour cream

Variation:

You could add mushrooms during the sauté phase if you choose. They would make a great addition.

1. Set the Instant Pot to Sauté and let it get hot. Add the oil.

2. Sauté the onion for 3 minutes.

3. Sprinkle each side of the pork chops with salt and pepper. Brown three of them at a time on each side in the Instant Pot. Remove them when done.

4. Pour in ½ cup of the broth and scrape the bottom of the pot, bringing up any stuck-on bits. Press Cancel.

5. Arrange the pork chops in the inner pot of the Instant Pot.

6. Pour the remaining broth, Worcestershire sauce, soy sauce, garlic powder, and onion powder over the chops.

7. Secure the lid and set the vent to sealing. Manually set the cook time for 8 minutes on high pressure.

8. When the cook time is over, let the pressure release naturally for 10 minutes, then manually release the remaining pressure.

9. When the pin drops, remove the lid. Switch the Instant Pot to Sauté.

10. Remove the chops and set aside.

11. Mix the cornstarch and cold water, then whisk into the sauce in the pot. Let thicken slightly for a few minutes. Press Cancel.

12. Before you add the sour cream to the sauce, let it cool for a few minutes, then slowly whisk it in. Serve the chops with the gravy over the top.

Golden Mushroom Pork Chops with Apples

Hope Comerford, Clinton Township, MI

Makes 4–6 servings

Prep. Time: 10 minutes ❧ *Cooking Time: 8–9 hours* ❧ *Ideal slow-cooker size: 5-qt.*

2 (10½-oz.) cans condensed golden mushroom soup

½ cup chicken stock

1 Tbsp. brown sugar

1 Tbsp. Worcestershire sauce

1 tsp. crushed dried thyme leaves

4 large Granny Smith apples, peeled and sliced

2 large onions, halved and sliced

2 lb. boneless pork chops

1. In the crock, mix the soup, chicken stock, brown sugar, Worcestershire, and thyme.

2. Add apples, onions, and pork. Toss together.

3. Cook on Low for 8–9 hours.

SLOW COOKER

Chops and Beans

Mary L. Casey, Scranton, PA

Makes 4–6 servings
Prep. Time: 15–20 minutes ⚜ *Cooking Time: 4–6 hours* ⚜ *Ideal slow-cooker size: 4-qt.*

2 (16-oz.) cans pork and beans
½ cup ketchup
2 slices bacon, browned and crumbled
½ cup chopped onions, sautéed
1 Tbsp. Worcestershire sauce
¼ cup firmly packed brown sugar
4–6 pork chops
2 tsp. prepared mustard
1 Tbsp. brown sugar
¼ cup ketchup
1 lemon, sliced

1. Combine beans, ½ cup ketchup, bacon, onions, Worcestershire sauce, and ¼ cup brown sugar in the slow cooker.

2. Brown chops in skillet. In separate bowl, mix 2 tsp. mustard, 1 Tbsp. brown sugar, and ¼ cup ketchup. Brush each chop with sauce, then carefully stack into cooker, placing a slice of lemon on each chop. Submerge in bean/bacon mixture.

3. Cover. Cook on Low for 4–6 hours.

Paprika Pork Chops with Rice

Sharon Easter, Yuba City, CA

Makes 4 servings
Prep. Time: 5 minutes ⚮ Cooking Time: 30 minutes

⅛ tsp. pepper

1 tsp. paprika

4–5 thick-cut boneless pork chops (1–1½ inches thick)

1 Tbsp. olive oil

1¼ cups water, *divided*

1 onion, sliced

½ green bell pepper, sliced in rings

1½ cups canned no-salt-added stewed tomatoes

1 cup brown rice

1. Mix the pepper and paprika in a flat dish. Dredge the chops in the seasoning mixture.

2. Set the Instant Pot to the Sauté function and heat the oil in the inner pot.

3. Brown the chops on both sides for 1 to 2 minutes a side. Remove the pork chops and set aside.

4. Pour a small amount of water into the inner pot and scrape up any bits from the bottom with a wooden spoon. Press Cancel.

5. Place the browned chops side by side in the inner pot. Place 1 slice onion and 1 ring of green pepper on top of each chop. Spoon tomatoes with their juices over the top.

6. Pour the rice in and pour the remaining water over the top.

7. Secure the lid and set the vent to sealing.

8. Manually set the cook time for 30 minutes on high pressure.

9. When the cooking time is over, manually release the pressure.

Barbecued Pork Chops

SLOW COOKER

Loretta Weisz, Auburn, WA

Makes 6 servings
Prep. Time: 10 minutes ⚘ *Cooking Time: 5–6 hours* ⚘ *Ideal slow-cooker size: 5-qt.*

4 loin pork chops, ¾ inch thick
1 cup ketchup
1 cup hot water
2 Tbsp. vinegar
1 Tbsp. Worcestershire sauce
2 tsp. brown sugar
½ tsp. pepper
½ tsp. chili powder
½ tsp. paprika

1. Place pork chops in the slow cooker.

2. Combine remaining ingredients. Pour over chops.

3. Cover. Cook on High for 5–6 hours, or until tender but not dry.

4. Cut chops in half and serve.

Salsa Verde Pork

Hope Comerford, Clinton Township, MI

Makes 6 servings
Prep. Time: 20 minutes ⚓ Cooking Time: 20 minutes

1½ lb. boneless pork loin

1 tsp. cumin

½ tsp. chili powder

1 large sweet onion, halved and sliced

4 garlic cloves, minced

14-oz. can diced tomatoes

16-oz. jar salsa verde (green salsa)

½ cup chicken stock

½ cup dry white wine (or use water or more stock)

1. Season the pork loin with the cumin and chili powder, then place it into the inner pot of the Instant Pot. Place the onion around the pork, then top with the garlic, diced tomatoes, salsa verde, chicken stock, and white wine.

2. Secure the lid and set the vent to sealing. Manually set the cook time for 20 minutes on high pressure.

3. When cook time is up, let the pressure release naturally for 10 minutes, then manually release any remaining pressure.

4. Break apart the pork with two forks and mix with contents of the inner pot.

Slow-Cooker Adaptation:

1. Place the pork loin in a 4-quart slow cooker and add the rest of the ingredients on top, omitting the chicken stock and white wine. Those ingredients are not needed in the slow cooker.

2. Cover and cook on Low for 6–6½ hours.

3. Break apart the pork with 2 forks and mix with contents of crock.

Carnitas

Hope Comerford, Clinton Township, MI

Makes 12 servings
Prep. Time: 10 minutes ⚶ *Cooking Time: 15 minutes*

1½ tsp. kosher salt

½ tsp. pepper

2 tsp. cumin

5 garlic cloves, minced

1 tsp. oregano

2 lb. pork shoulder roast

3 bay leaves

2 cups gluten-free chicken stock

2 Tbsp. lime juice

1 tsp. lime zest

12 (6-inch) gluten-free white corn tortillas

1. Mix together the salt, pepper, cumin, garlic, and oregano. Rub it onto the pork roast.

2. Place the pork roast into the inner pot of the Instant Pot. Place the bay leaves around the pork roast, then pour in the chicken stock around the roast, being careful not to wash off the spices.

3. Secure the lid and set the vent to sealing. Manually set the cook time for 15 minutes on high pressure.

4. When cook time is up, let the pressure release naturally.

5. Add the lime juice and lime zest to the inner pot and stir. You may choose to shred the pork if you wish.

6. Serve on the white corn tortillas

Slow-Cooker Adaptation:

1. Place pork shoulder roast in a 4-quart slow cooker.
2. Mix together the salt, pepper, cumin, garlic, and oregano. Rub it onto the pork roast.
3. Place the bay leaves around the pork roast, then pour in the chicken stock around the roast, being careful not to wash off the spices.
4. Cover and cook on Low for 10–12 hours.
5. Remove the roast with a slotted spoon, as well as the bay leaves. Shred the pork between 2 forks, then replace the shredded pork in the crock and stir.
6. Add the lime juice and lime zest to the crock and stir.
7. Serve on warmed white corn tortillas.

SLOW COOKER

Zesty Pork Burritos

Hope Comerford, Clinton Township, MI

Makes 8–10 servings
Prep. Time: 5 minutes ❧ Cooking Time: 8–10 hours ❧ Ideal slow-cooker size: 3-qt.

3–4-lb. pork shoulder

14½-oz. can diced tomatoes with green chilies

1-oz. pkg. low-sodium taco seasoning

2 tsp. honey

Flour tortillas

Burrito fixings:

Shredded cheese, *optional*

Lettuce, *optional*

Sour cream, *optional*

Refried beans, *optional*

1. Place all ingredients in crock (except tortillas and optional fixings).

2. Cover and cook on Low for 8–10 hours.

3. Remove pork and shred it between two forks. Stir it back through the juices.

4. Serve in tortillas with optional toppings, rolled up as burritos.

Simple Shredded Pork Tacos

Jennifer Freed, Rockingham, AL

Makes 6 servings
Prep. Time: 5 minutes ♣ Cooking Time: 8 hours ♣ Ideal slow-cooker size: 4-qt.

2-lb. boneless pork roast
1 cup salsa
4-oz. can chopped green chilies
½ tsp. garlic salt
½ tsp. pepper

1. Place all ingredients in the slow cooker.

2. Cover; cook on Low for 8 hours, or until meat is tender.

3. To serve, use two forks to shred pork.

Serving suggestion:
Serve with taco shells and your favorite taco fixings.

Barbecue Pork Sandwiches

Carol Eveleth, Cheyenne, WY

Makes 4 servings
Prep. Time: 20 minutes ⚜ *Cooking Time: 1 hour*

2 tsp. salt

1 tsp. onion powder

1 tsp. garlic powder

2-lb. pork shoulder roast, cut into
3-inch pieces

1 Tbsp. olive oil

2 cups barbecue sauce

1. In a small bowl, combine the salt, onion powder, and garlic powder. Season the pork with the rub.

2. Turn the Instant Pot on to Sauté. Heat the olive oil in the inner pot.

3. Add the pork to the oil and turn to coat. Lock the lid and set vent to sealing.

4. Press Manual and cook on high pressure for 45 minutes.

5. When cooking is complete, release the pressure manually, then open the lid.

6. Using two forks, shred the pork, pour barbecue sauce over the pork, then press Sauté. Simmer, 3 to 5 minutes. Press Cancel. Toss pork to mix.

Serving suggestion:

Pile the shredded barbecue pork on the bottom half of a bun. Add more toppings if you wish, then finish with the top half of the bun.

Eggroll Bowl

Hope Comerford, Clinton Township, MI

Makes 4 servings
Prep. Time: 10 minutes ⚬ Cooking Time: 3 minutes

1 Tbsp. sesame oil

1 lb. ground pork (or ground chicken, turkey, shrimp, tofu, black beans, crumbles, etc.)

1 small onion, halved and sliced into half rings

4 garlic cloves, minced

⅓ cup chicken or vegetable stock

1 tsp. ground ginger

¼ tsp. pepper

⅓ cup coconut aminos

¼ cup rice vinegar

16 oz. bag tricolor shredded coleslaw

3 Tbsp. chopped green onions, *optional*

½ tsp. sesame seeds, *optional*

1. Pour the sesame oil into the inner pot of the Instant Pot and press Sauté.

2. Add the ground pork and begin to brown for 4–5 minutes.

3. When the meat is mostly browned, add the onion and garlic and continue to sauté for another 2–3 minutes.

4. Deglaze the pot with the stock, scraping the bottom well, then press Cancel.

5. Add the ginger, pepper, coconut aminos, rice vinegar, and end with the coleslaw on top.

6. Secure the lid and set the cook time for 3 minutes on high pressure.

7. When cook time is up, manually release the pressure. When the pin drops, remove the lid and stir.

8. Distribute the contents of the inner pot among four bowls, then top with the optional chopped green onions and sesame seeds. Enjoy!

Serving suggestion:
You could serve this with some crispy fried wontons on the side, or over cauliflower rice.

Beer Poached Italian Sausage

Hope Comerford, Clinton Township, MI

Makes 4–5 servings
Prep. Time: 5 minutes   &   Cooking Time: 6–7 hours   &   Ideal slow-cooker size: 3-qt.

1 lb. sweet Italian sausage
12 oz. beer of your choice
Hot dog buns

1. Place the Italian sausage in crock and pour the beer over the top.

2. Cover and cook on Low for 6–7 hours.

3. Serve in the hot dog buns with toppings of your choice.

Instant Pot Adaptation:

1. Set the Instant Pot to the Sauté function and melt 2 Tbsp. butter (notice the addition of the ingredient).

2. Brown the Italian sausage in the butter, then press Cancel on the Instant Pot. Remove the sausage and set aside.

3. Pour ¼ cup beer in the inner pot and deglaze the bottom of it by scraping up any stuck-on bits.

4. Place the metal trivet into the inner pot and put the sausages on the rack.

5. Secure the lid and set the vent to sealing. Set the cook time for 6 minutes on high pressure.

6. When cook time is up, let the pressure release naturally for 10 minutes, then manually release any remaining pressure. When the pin drops, remove the lid.

7. Serve in the hot dog buns with toppings of your choice.

Polish Sausage and Sauerkraut

Hope Comerford, Clinton Township, MI

Makes 4–6 servings
Prep. Time: 25 minutes ♣ *Cooking Time: 6–7 hours* ♣ *Ideal slow-cooker size: 6-qt.*

27 oz. Polish sausage, cut into 1½-inch angled pieces

4 slices of cooked bacon, chopped

2 Golden Delicious apples, peeled and cut into thin slices

2 lb. sauerkraut, rinsed well and drained

½ of a large red onion, sliced

1 bay leaf

2 garlic cloves, minced

2 Tbsp. brown sugar

12 oz. dark beer

1. Place all the ingredients into the crock, pouring the beer in last.

2. Cover and cook on Low for 6–7 hours.

3. When you are ready to serve, remove the bay leaf and discard it.

Beef Main Dishes

Coca-Cola Roast

SLOW COOKER INSTANT POT ADAPTATION

Hope Comerford, Clinton Township, MI

Makes 6 servings
Prep. Time: 10 minutes ❧ Cooking Time: 8–10 hours ❧ Ideal slow-cooker size: 6-qt.

3–4 lb. boneless bottom round steak

5–6 small potatoes, cut if you'd like

4–5 medium carrots, peeled, cut in half or thirds

2–3 garlic cloves, chopped

Salt to taste

Pepper to taste

12-oz. can Coca-Cola

1. Place roast in crock.

2. Place potatoes and carrots around roast.

3. Sprinkle roast and veggies with the garlic, salt, and pepper.

4. Pour the can of Coca-Cola over the top.

5. Cover and cook on Low for 8–10 hours.

Instant Pot Adaptation:

1. Set the Instant Pot to the Sauté function and heat up 1 Tbsp. oil of your choice. (Notice the addition of the ingredient.)

2. Cut the meat into three equal pieces and sprinkle with salt and pepper. Brown both sides, then set aside.

3. Pour in ½ cup water (notice the addition of the ingredient) and scrape up any stuck-on bits. Press Cancel.

4. Place the meat back in the inner pot, along with the carrots and garlic. Pour in the Coca-Cola.

5. Secure the lid and set the vent to sealing. Set the cook time for 55 minutes on high pressure.

6. When cook time is up, let the pressure release naturally for at least 10 minutes, then manually release the remaining pressure.

Smoky Brisket

Angeline Lang, Greeley, CO

Makes 8–10 servings
Prep. Time: 5 minutes   ❧   Cooking Time: 10–12 hours   ❧   Ideal slow-cooker size: 4½- to 5-qt.

2 medium onions, sliced
3–4-lb. beef brisket
I Tbsp. smoke-flavored salt
I tsp. celery seed
I Tbsp. mustard seed
½ tsp. pepper
12-oz. bottle chili sauce

1. Arrange onions in bottom of slow cooker.

2. Sprinkle both sides of meat with smoke-flavored salt.

3. Combine celery seed, mustard seed, pepper, and chili sauce. Pour over meat.

4. Cover. Cook on Low for 10–12 hours.

Barbecued Brisket

Dorothy Dyer, Lee's Summit, MO

Makes 9–12 servings
Prep. Time: 10 minutes ⚬ Cooking Time: 70 minutes

1 cup beef broth
⅓ cup Italian salad dressing
1½ tsp. liquid smoke
⅓ cup + 2 tsp. brown sugar, packed
½ tsp. celery salt
½ tsp. salt
1 Tbsp. Worcestershire sauce
½ tsp. pepper
¼ tsp. chili powder
½ tsp. garlic powder
3–4-lb. beef brisket
1¼ cups barbecue sauce
Sandwich rolls

1. Pour the beef broth, Italian dressing, liquid smoke, brown sugar, celery salt, salt, Worcestershire sauce, pepper, chili powder, and garlic powder into the inner pot of the Instant Pot. Stir. Place the brisket into the broth mixture. You may cut it into pieces if needed for it to fit under the broth.

2. Secure the lid and set the vent to sealing. Manually set the cook time for 70 minutes on high pressure.

3. When the cook time is over, let the pressure release naturally.

4. Lift the meat out of the Instant Pot and shred it in a bowl. Pour the barbecue sauce over the meat and stir. Serve on sandwich rolls.

Barbacoa Beef

Cindy Herren, West Des Moines, IA

Makes 6–8 servings
Prep. Time: 20 minutes   Cooking Time: 60 minutes

5 garlic cloves

½ medium onion

Juice of 1 lime

2–4 Tbsp. chipotles in adobo sauce (to taste)

1 tsp. ground cumin

1 tsp. ground oregano

½ tsp. ground cloves

1 cup water

3 lb. beef eye of round or bottom round roast, all fat trimmed

2½ tsp. kosher salt

Pepper

1 tsp. oil

3 bay leaves

½ tsp. salt, *optional*

½ tsp. cumin, *optional*

1. Place the garlic, onion, lime juice, chipotles, cumin, oregano, cloves, and water in a blender and puree until smooth.

2. Trim all the fat off the meat and then cut the meat into 3-inch pieces. Season with the salt and pepper.

3. Set the Instant Pot to Sauté. When hot; add the oil and brown the meat, in batches on all sides, about 5 minutes.

4. Press Cancel. Add all of the browned meat, sauce from the blender, and bay leaves to the inner pot.

5. Secure the lid and set the vent to sealing.

6. Cook on high pressure for 60 minutes.

7. Manually release the pressure once cook time is up.

8. Remove the meat and place in a dish. Shred with two forks, and reserve 1½ cups of the liquid. Discard the bay leaves and the remaining liquid.

9. Return the shredded meat to the pot, add ½ tsp. salt (or to taste), ½ tsp. cumin, and the 1½ cups of the reserved liquid.

Serving suggestion:
Serve with fresh salsa, sour cream, and corn over rice.

Slow-Cooker Adaptation:

1. Trim the roast of fat and place it into a 5-quart slow cooker. Season with the salt and pepper.

2. Place the garlic, onion, lime juice, chipotles, cumin, oregano, cloves, and water in a blender and puree until smooth. Pour this over the roast. Add the bay leaf.

3. Cover and cook on Low for 8–10 hours.

4. Continue with step 8 above.

Chili-Lime Mexican Shredded Beef

Genelle Taylor, Perrysburg, OH

Makes 6–8 servings
Prep. Time: 10 minutes ⚬ *Cooking Time: 8 hours* ⚬ *Ideal slow-cooker size: 5- to 6-qt.*

2–3-lb. beef chuck roast
4 cups lemon-lime soda
1 tsp. chili powder
1 tsp. salt
3 garlic cloves, crushed
2 limes, juiced

1. Place the roast in the slow cooker.

2. Pour soda over roast.

3. Season with chili powder, salt, and garlic.

4. Cover and cook on Low for 8 hours.

5. Shred the beef, return to crock, pour lime juice over, and stir.

Serving suggestion:

Serve hot, with black beans and rice, or use in tacos.

Instant Pot Boneless Short Ribs

Hope Comerford, Clinton Township, MI

Makes 4 servings
Prep. Time: 10 minutes & Cooking Time: 50 minutes plus 3–5 minutes

3 lb. boneless short ribs
1 Tbsp. oil
½ tsp. salt
⅛ tsp. pepper
1 cup beef stock
1 large onion, sliced
4 carrots, cut into 2-inch chunks
6 garlic cloves, smashed
¼ cup balsamic vinegar
¾ cup red wine
1 sprig rosemary
1 sprig thyme
2 Tbsp. cold water
2 Tbsp. cornstarch

1. Set the Instant Pot to Sauté and heat the oil. Season the ribs with the salt and pepper, then brown them on each side. Set aside.

2. Pour in ½ cup of the beef stock and deglaze the inner pot, scraping up any stuck-on bits. Press Cancel.

3. Place the ribs back in the inner pot, then add the onion, carrots, garlic, balsamic vinegar, red wine, remaining stock, rosemary, and thyme.

4. Secure the lid and set the vent to sealing. Manually set the cook time for 50 minutes on high pressure.

5. When cook time is up, let the pressure release naturally for 20 minutes, then manually release the remaining pressure.

6. Switch the Instant Pot to the Sauté function.

7. Mix the cold water and cornstarch. Gently stir this mixture into the contents of the inner pot and let simmer until the sauce is thickened a bit, about 3–5 minutes.

8. Serve the short ribs and carrots with the sauce spooned over the top.

Serving suggestion:
Serve with mashed or baked potatoes.

Chianti-Braised Short Ribs

Veronica Sabo, Shelton, CT

Makes 8 servings
Prep. Time: 30–40 minutes   Cooking Time: 6 hours   Ideal slow-cooker size: 5- or 6-qt.

8 meaty beef short ribs on bone
(4–5 lb.)
Salt to taste
Pepper to taste
I Tbsp. olive oil
I onion, finely chopped
2 cups Chianti
2 tomatoes, seeded and chopped
I tsp. tomato paste

1. Season ribs with salt and pepper.

2. Add olive oil to large skillet. Brown half the ribs 7–10 minutes, turning to brown all sides. Drain and remove to slow cooker.

3. Repeat browning with second half of ribs. Drain and transfer to slow cooker.

4. Pour off all but 1 tablespoon drippings from skillet.

5. Sauté onion in skillet, scraping up any browned bits, until slightly softened, about 4 minutes.

6. Add wine and tomatoes to skillet. Bring to a boil.

7. Carefully pour hot mixture into slow cooker.

8. Cover. Cook on Low for 6 hours, or until ribs are tender.

9. Transfer ribs to serving plate and cover to keep warm.

10. Strain cooking liquid from slow cooker into a measuring cup.

11. Skim off as much fat as possible.

12. Pour remaining juice into skillet used to brown ribs. Boil sauce until reduced to 1 cup.

13. Stir in tomato paste until smooth.

14. Season to taste with salt and pepper.

15. Serve sauce over ribs or on the side.

Swiss Steak with Onion, Peppers, and Tomatoes

Nadine Martinitz, Salina, KS
Hazel L. Propst, Oxford, PA

Makes 10 servings
Prep. Time: 30 minutes ❧ Cooking Time: 6–8 hours ❧ Ideal slow-cooker size: 5- or 6-qt.

3-lb. lean round steak
⅓ cup flour
2 tsp. kosher salt
½ tsp. pepper
2 Tbsp. olive oil
1 large onion, or more, sliced
1 large bell pepper, or more, sliced
14½-oz. can low-sodium stewed tomatoes, or 3–4 fresh tomatoes, chopped
Water

1. Cut meat into 10 pieces. Pound both sides. Mix the flour, salt, and pepper. Dredge each piece of meat on both sides in flavored flour.

2. Sauté meat in oil over medium heat in skillet, until browned. Transfer to slow cooker.

3. Brown onion and pepper in pan drippings. Add tomatoes and bring to boil. Stir pan drippings loose. Pour over steak. Add water to completely cover steak.

4. Cover. Cook on Low for 6–8 hours.

Variations:

To add some flavor, stir your favorite dried herbs into Step 3. Or add fresh herbs just before serving.

Three-Pepper Steak

Renee Hankins, Narvon, PA

Makes 10 servings
Prep. Time: 15 minutes ☙ Cooking Time: 15 minutes

3-lb. beef flank steak, cut in ¼–½-inch-thick slices across the grain

3 bell peppers—one red, one orange, and one yellow pepper (or any combination of colors), cut into ¼-inch-thick slices

2 garlic cloves, sliced

1 large onion, sliced

1 tsp. ground cumin

½ tsp. dried oregano

1 bay leaf

¼ cup water

Salt to taste

14½-oz. can diced tomatoes in juice

Jalapeño peppers, sliced, *optional*

1. Place all ingredients into the Instant Pot and stir.

2. Sprinkle with jalapeño pepper slices if you wish.

3. Secure the lid and make sure vent is set to sealing. Press Manual and set the time for 15 minutes.

4. When cook time is up, let the pressure release naturally for 15 minutes, then perform a quick release of the remaining pressure.

Serving suggestion:

We love this served over noodles, rice, or torn tortillas.

Slow-Cooker Adaptation:

1. In a 4–5-quart slow cooker, place sliced peppers, garlic, onion, cumin, oregano, and bay leaf in the slow cooker. Stir gently to mix.

2. Put steak slices on top of vegetable mixture. Season with salt.

3. Spoon tomatoes with juice over top. Sprinkle with jalapeño pepper slices if you wish. *Do not stir.*

4. Cover. Cook on low for 5–8 hours, depending on the slow cooker. Check after 5 hours to see if meat is tender. If not, continue cooking until tender but not dry.

Philly Cheese Steaks

Michele Ruvola, Vestal, NY

Makes 6 servings
Prep. Time: 15 minutes ⚜ Cooking Time: 55 minutes

I red pepper, sliced
I green pepper, sliced
I onion, sliced
2 garlic cloves, minced
2½ lb. thinly sliced steak
I tsp. salt
½ tsp. pepper
0.7-oz. pkg. dry Italian dressing mix
I cup water
I beef bouillon cube
6 slices of provolone cheese
6 hoagie rolls

1. Put all ingredients in the inner pot of the Instant Pot, except the provolone cheese and rolls.

2. Seal the lid, make sure vent is at sealing, and cook for 40 minutes on the Slow Cook setting.

3. Let the pressure release naturally for 10 minutes, then do a quick release.

4. Scoop meat and vegetables into rolls.

5. Top with provolone cheese and put on a baking sheet.

6. Broil in oven for 5 minutes.

7. Pour remaining juice in pot into cups for dipping.

Flavorful French Dip

Marcella Stalter, Flanagan, IL

Makes 8 servings

Prep. Time: 5 minutes ⚘ *Cooking Time: 5–6 hours* ⚘ *Ideal slow-cooker size: 3½-qt.*

3-lb. chuck roast

2 cups water

½ cup soy sauce

I tsp. dried rosemary

I tsp. dried thyme

I tsp. garlic powder

I bay leaf

3–4 whole peppercorns

1. Place roast in the slow cooker. Add water, soy sauce, and seasonings.

2. Cover. Cook on High for 5–6 hours, or until beef is tender.

3. Remove beef from broth. Shred with fork. Keep warm.

4. Strain broth. Skim fat. Pour broth into small cups for dipping.

Serving suggestion:

Serve beef on French rolls.

Instant Pot Adaptation:

1. Mix the rosemary, thyme, and garlic powder. Rub this all over the roast in the inner pot of the Instant Pot.

2. Pour in the peppercorns, soy sauce, and water.

3. Secure the lid and set the vent to sealing. Set the cook time for 45 minutes on high pressure.

4. When the cook time is up, let the pressure release naturally. When the pin drops, remove the lid.

5. Continue to steps 3 and 4 above.

Taco Meatloaf

Tammy Smith, Dorchester, WI

Makes 8 servings

Prep. Time: 20 minutes ⚜ *Cooking Time: 4 hours* ⚜ *Ideal slow-cooker size: oval 5- or 6-qt.*

3 eggs, lightly beaten

½ cup crushed tomatoes

¾ cup crushed tortilla chips

I medium onion, finely chopped

2 garlic cloves, minced

3 tsp. taco seasoning

2 tsp. chili powder

I lb. ground beef

I lb. ground pork

½ tsp. salt

¾ tsp. pepper

1. Grease interior of slow-cooker crock.

2. Make a tinfoil sling for the slow cooker so you can lift the cooked meatloaf out easily. Begin by folding a strip of foil accordion-fashion so that it's about 1½–2 inches wide, and long enough to fit from the top edge of the crock, down inside and up the other side, plus a 2-inch overhang on each side of the cooker. Make a second strip exactly like the first.

3. Place one strip in crock, running from end to end. Place second strip in crock, running from side to side. The strips should form a cross in bottom of the crock.

4. In a large bowl, combine all ingredients well.

5. Shape into a loaf. Place into crock so that the center of loaf sits where the two strips of foil cross.

6. Cover. Cook for 4 hours on Low.

7. Using the foil handles, lift loaf onto platter. Cover to keep warm. Let stand for 10–15 minutes before slicing.

Stuffed Bell Peppers

Mary Puterbaugh, Elwood, IN

Makes 8 servings
Prep. Time: 20 minutes   Cooking Time: 5–11 hours   Ideal slow-cooker size: 6- to 7-qt.

2 lb. ground beef, lightly browned

1 large onion, chopped

1 cup cooked rice

2 eggs, beaten

½ cup milk

½ cup ketchup

Dash hot pepper sauce

2 tsp. salt

½ tsp. pepper

8 large bell peppers, capped and seeded

1. Combine all ingredients except peppers. Gently pack mixture into peppers. Place in greased slow cooker.

2. Cover. Cook on Low for 9–11 hours, or on High for 5–6 hours.

Swedish Cabbage Rolls

Jean Butzer, Batavia, NY
Pam Hochstedler, Kalona, IA

Makes 6 servings
Prep. Time: 25 minutes & Cooking Time: 7–9 hours & Ideal slow-cooker size: 2- to 4-qt.

12 large cabbage leaves
1 egg, beaten
¼ cup fat-free milk
¼ cup finely chopped onions
1 tsp. sea salt
¼ tsp. pepper
1 lb. extra-lean ground beef, browned and drained
1 cup cooked brown rice
8-oz. can low-sodium tomato sauce
1 Tbsp. brown sugar
1 Tbsp. lemon juice
1 tsp. Worcestershire sauce

1. Immerse cabbage leaves in boiling water for about 3 minutes or until limp. Drain.

2. Combine egg, milk, onions, salt, pepper, beef, and rice. Place about ¼ cup meat mixture in center of each leaf. Fold in sides and roll ends over meat. Place in the slow cooker.

3. Combine tomato sauce, brown sugar, lemon juice, and Worcestershire sauce. Pour over cabbage rolls.

4. Cover. Cook on Low for 7–9 hours.

Enchilada Casserole

Hope Comerford, Clinton Township, MI

Makes 8 servings
Prep. Time: 25 minutes & Cooking Time: 4–6 hours & Ideal slow-cooker size: 6-qt.

9 small round flour tortillas, *divided*

1½ lb. ground beef, browned, *divided*

1 medium onion, chopped, *divided*

2 cups fresh diced tomatoes, *divided*

10-oz. can mild red enchilada sauce, *divided*

2 cups shredded Mexican blend cheese, *divided*

10-oz. can mild green enchilada sauce

1. Spray crock with nonstick spray.

2. Place 3 tortillas in bottom of crock. Cut them if necessary to make them fit.

3. Layer ½ of ground beef on top, followed by ½ the onion, ½ the diced tomatoes, ½ the red enchilada sauce, and ⅓ of the cheese. Repeat this process once more.

4. Finish with final 3 tortillas on top, entire can of green enchilada sauce, and remaining cheese.

5. Cook on Low for 4–6 hours.

Walking Tacos

Hope Comerford, Clinton Township, MI

Makes 10–16 servings
Prep. Time: 10 minutes   Cooking Time: 6–7 hours   Ideal slow-cooker size: 2–3 qt.

2 lb. ground beef

2 tsp. garlic powder

2 tsp. onion powder

1 Tbsp. cumin

2 Tbsp. chili powder

1 tsp. salt

½ tsp. oregano

½ tsp. red pepper flakes

1 small onion, minced

1 clove garlic, minced

10–16 individual-sized bags of Doritos

Suggested toppings:

Diced tomatoes

Shredded cheese

Diced cucumbers

Chopped onion

Shredded lettuce

Sour cream

Salsa

1. Crumble the ground beef into the crock.

2. In a bowl, mix all the spices, onion, and garlic. Pour this over beef, then stir it up.

3. Cover and cook for 6–7 hours, breaking it up occasionally.

4. Remove some of the grease if you wish.

5. To serve, open the bag of Doritos, crumble the chips in the bag with your hand, add some of the ground beef to the bag, then any additional toppings you desire. Serve each bag with a fork.

INSTANT POT

Spaghetti and Meatballs

Hope Comerford, Clinton Township, MI

Makes 8 servings
Prep. Time: 10 minutes ⚘ Cooking Time: 3 minutes

1 Tbsp. olive oil
1 small onion, chopped
3 cups water, *divided*
15-oz. can crushed tomatoes
8-oz. can tomato sauce
1½ tsp. Italian seasoning
1 tsp. garlic powder
1 tsp. onion powder
1 tsp. sea salt
¼ tsp. pepper
12 oz. frozen meatballs
12 oz. spaghetti noodles, broken in half

1. Set the Instant Pot to the Sauté function and heat the olive oil.

2. When the oil is hot, sauté the onion for 3 to 5 minutes, or until translucent.

3. Pour in 1 cup of the water and scrape any bits from the bottom of the inner pot with a wooden spoon or spatula.

4. In a bowl, mix the crushed tomatoes, tomato sauce, Italian seasoning, garlic powder, onion powder, sea salt, and pepper. Pour 1 cup of this in the inner pot and stir.

5. Pour in the meatballs and arrange the spaghetti in the pot. Press it down so it's in there evenly, but *do not stir*.

6. Pour the remaining pasta sauce evenly over the top. Again, *do not stir*.

7. Secure the lid and set the vent to sealing. Manually set the cook time for 3 minutes.

8. When the cook time is over, let the pressure release naturally for 10 minutes, then manually release the remaining pressure.

9. When the pin drops, remove the lid and stir. This will thicken as it sits a bit.

Sloppy Joes

Hope Comerford, Clinton Township, MI

Makes 15–18 servings

Prep. Time: 25 minutes ☙ Cooking Time: 6–7 hours ☙ Ideal slow-cooker size: 6-qt.

1½ lb. extra-lean ground beef

16 oz. ground turkey sausage

½ large red onion, chopped

½ green bell pepper, chopped

8-oz. can low-sodium tomato sauce

½ cup water

½ cup ketchup

¼ cup tightly packed brown sugar

2 Tbsp. apple cider vinegar

2 Tbsp. yellow mustard

1 Tbsp. Worcestershire sauce

1 Tbsp. chili powder

1 tsp. garlic powder

1 tsp. onion powder

¼ tsp. salt

¼ tsp. pepper

1. Brown the ground beef and sausage in a pan. Drain all grease.

2. While the beef and sausage are cooking, mix together the remaining ingredients in the crock.

3. Add the cooked beef and sausage to the crock and mix.

4. Cover and cook on Low for 6–7 hours.

Serving suggestion:
Serve on hamburger buns.

Easy Hamburgers

Hope Comerford, Clinton Township, MI

Makes 8–9 3-inch patties
Prep. Time: 20 minutes ⚬ *Cooking Time: 4–5 hours* ⚬ *Ideal slow-cooker size: 6- to 7-qt.*

¼ cup water

2 lb. ground beef

1 cup Italian seasoned bread crumbs

1-oz. pkg. Hidden Valley Ranch Salad Dressing and Seasoning Mix

1-oz. pkg. Lipton Onion Soup Mix

1 egg

1 Tbsp. Worcestershire sauce

1. Crumple up some foil in the bottom of the crock. This will keep the burgers from cooking in the grease. Pour the water into the bottom of the crock.

2. In a bowl, mix the ground beef, bread crumbs, ranch dressing mix, onion soup mix, egg, and Worcestershire sauce. Form the burgers into 3-inch patties.

3. Place enough patties onto the crumpled foil that just covers the bottom. Do not overlap the patties.

4. Fold some foil into strips and make a star shape, crisscrossing them over one another, on top of the patties already in the crock. Lay the remaining patties on top.

5. Cover and cook on Low for 4–5 hours.

Meatless & Seafood Main Dishes

Eggplant Parmesan Lightened Up

Hope Comerford, Clinton Township, MI

Makes 4 servings
Prep. Time: 15 minutes & Cooking Time: 10 minutes

I large eggplant

Salt

I cup water

Nonstick cooking spray

2 cups low-sodium, low-sugar marinara sauce, *divided*

½ tsp. dried basil

¾ cup shredded Parmesan cheese

1. Prepare the eggplant by cutting the top and bottom off, then slicing it in long ¼-inch-thick slices. Lay the slices out on a baking sheet and sprinkle them with salt on both sides. Let them sit for a few minutes and then pat each side dry with a paper towel.

2. Pour the water into the inner pot of the Instant Pot and place the trivet on top.

3. Spray a 7-inch round baking pan with nonstick cooking spray.

4. Spread about ½ cup of marinara sauce on the bottom of the baking dish.

5. Begin layering the eggplant, a little marinara sauce, a sprinkle of basil, and a sprinkle of Parmesan until you have no more eggplant. End with sauce, a final sprinkle of basil, and Parmesan.

6. Secure the lid and set the vent to sealing.

7. Manually set the cook time to 10 minutes at high pressure.

8. When the cooking time is over, manually release the pressure.

9. When the pin drops, remove the lid and carefully remove the trivet with oven mitts. Allow to cool a bit before serving.

SLOW COOKER

Vegetable Stuffed Peppers

Shirley Hinh, Wayland, IA

Makes 8 servings
Prep. Time: 20 minutes ⚘ Cooking Time: 6–8 hour
Ideal slow-cooker size: 6-qt. (large enough so that all peppers sit on the bottom of the cooker)

4 large green, red, or yellow bell
peppers

½ cup quick-cooking rice

¼ cup minced onion

¼ cup sliced black olives

2 tsp. light soy sauce

¼ tsp. pepper

I clove garlic, minced

28-oz. can low-sodium whole tomatoes

6-oz. can low-sodium tomato paste

15¼-oz. can corn or kidney beans,
drained

1. Cut tops off peppers (reserve) and remove seeds. Stand peppers up in the slow cooker.

2. Mix remaining ingredients in a bowl. Stuff peppers. (You'll have leftover filling.)

3. Place pepper tops back on peppers. Pour remaining filling over the stuffed peppers and work down in between the peppers.

4. Cover. Cook on Low for 6–8 hours, or until the peppers are done to your liking.

5. If you prefer, you may add ½ cup tomato juice if recipe is too dry.

6. Cut peppers in half and serve.

Honey Lemon Garlic Salmon

Judy Gascho, Woodburn, OR

Makes 4 servings
Prep. Time: 15 minutes   ♣   Cooking Time: 8 minutes

5 Tbsp. olive oil

3 Tbsp. honey

2–3 Tbsp. lemon juice

3 garlic cloves, minced

4 (3–4-oz.) fresh salmon fillets

Salt to taste

Pepper to taste

1–2 Tbsp. minced parsley (dried or fresh)

Lemon slices, *optional*

1. Mix olive oil, honey, lemon juice, and minced garlic in a bowl.

2. Place each piece of salmon on a piece of foil big enough to wrap up the piece of fish.

3. Brush each fillet generously with the olive oil mixture.

4. Sprinkle with salt, pepper, and parsley flakes.

5. Top each with a thin slice of lemon, if desired.

6. Wrap each fillet and seal well at top.

7. Place 1½ cups of water in the inner pot of the Instant Pot and place the trivet in the pot.

8. Place wrapped fillets on the trivet.

9. Close the lid and turn valve to sealing.

10. Cook on Manual at high pressure for 5–8 minutes for smaller pieces, or 10–12 minutes if they are large.

11. When cook time is over, manually release the pressure.

12. Unwrap and enjoy.

Metric Equivalent Measurements

If you're accustomed to using metric measurements, I don't want you to be inconvenienced by the imperial measurements I use in this book.

Use this handy chart, too, to figure out the size of the slow cooker you'll need for each recipe.

Weight (Dry Ingredients)

1 oz		30 g
4 oz	¼ lb	120 g
8 oz	½ lb	240 g
12 oz	¾ lb	360 g
16 oz	1 lb	480 g
32 oz	2 lb	960 g

Slow-Cooker Sizes

1-quart	0.96 l
2-quart	1.92 l
3-quart	2.88 l
4-quart	3.84 l
5-quart	4.80 l
6-quart	5.76 l
7-quart	6.72 l
8-quart	7.68 l

Volume (Liquid Ingredients)

½ tsp.		2 ml
1 tsp.		5 ml
1 Tbsp.	½ fl oz	15 ml
2 Tbsp.	1 fl oz	30 ml
¼ cup	2 fl oz	60 ml
⅓ cup	3 fl oz	80 ml
½ cup	4 fl oz	120 ml
⅔ cup	5 fl oz	160 ml
¾ cup	6 fl oz	180 ml
1 cup	8 fl oz	240 ml
1 pt	16 fl oz	480 ml
1 qt	32 fl oz	960 ml

Length

¼ in	6 mm
½ in	13 mm
¾ in	19 mm
1 in	25 mm
6 in	15 cm
12 in	30 cm

Recipe & Ingredient Index

About the Author

Hope Comerford is a mom, wife, elementary music teacher, blogger, recipe developer, public speaker, Young Living Essential Oils essential oil enthusiast/educator, and published author. In 2013, she was diagnosed with a severe gluten intolerance and since then has spent many hours creating easy, practical, and delicious gluten-free recipes that can be enjoyed by both those who are affected by gluten and those who are not.

Growing up, Hope spent many hours in the kitchen with her Meme (grandmother), and her love for cooking grew from there. While working on her master's degree when her daughter was young, Hope turned to her slow cookers for some salvation and sanity. It was from there she began truly experimenting with recipes and quickly learned she had the ability to get a little more creative in the kitchen and develop her own recipes.

In 2010, Hope started her blog, *A Busy Mom's Slow Cooker Adventures*, to simply share the recipes she was making with her family and friends. She never imagined people all over the world would begin visiting her page and sharing her recipes with others as well. In 2013, Hope self-published her first cookbook, *Slow Cooker Recipes: 10 Ingredients or Less and Gluten-Free*, and then later wrote *The Gluten-Free Slow Cooker*.

Hope became the new brand ambassador and author of Fix-It and Forget-It in mid-2016. Since then, she has brought her excitement and creativeness to the Fix-It and Forget-It brand. Through Fix-It and Forget-It, she has written *Fix-It and Forget-It Comfort Foods Cookbook*, *Fix-It and Forget-It Slow Cooker Freezer Meals Cookbook*, *Fix-It and Forget-It Freezer to Instant Pot Cookbook*, *Welcome Home 30-Minute Meals*, *Fix-It and Forget-It Healthy One-Pot Meals*, and many more.

Hope lives in the city of Clinton Township, Michigan, near Metro Detroit. She has been happily married to her husband and best friend, Justin, since 2008. Together they have two children, Ella and Gavin, who are her motivation, inspiration, and heart. In her spare time, Hope enjoys traveling, singing, cooking, reading books, working on wooden puzzles, spending time with friends and family, and relaxing.